Also by Leslie Levine

Will This Place Ever Feel Like Home
Ice Cream for Breakfast

wish it, dream it, do it

Turn the Life You're Living into the Life You Want

~ Leslie Levine ~

A Fireside Book

Published by Simon & Schuster

New York   London   Toronto   Sydney

FIRESIDE
Rockefeller Center
1230 Avenue of the Americas
New York, NY 10020

FIRESIDE and colophon are registered trademarks
of Simon & Schuster, Inc.

For information regarding special discounts for bulk purchases,
please contact Simon & Schuster Special Sales at 1-800-456-6798
or business@simonandschuster.com

Designed by Jaime Putorti

Manufactured in the United States of America

10   9   8   7   6   5   4   3   2

Library of Congress Cataloging-in-Publication Data
Levine, Leslie.
    Wish it, dream it, do it: turn the life you're living into the life
you want / Leslie Levine.
        p.   cm.
    "A Fireside book".
    Includes bibliographical references.
    1. Success—Psychological aspects. 2. Self-actualization
    (Psychology). I. Title.
BF637.S8L449   2004   158.1—dc22   2003057341
ISBN 0-7432-2981-9

To the memory of Helen and Jerry Levine

And for Jon, Esther, and Philip.

With love always.

Acknowledgments

*F*irst, many thanks to Danielle Egan-Miller, cherished friend, sage adviser, and humble life-changer. I also wish to thank my agent, Joëlle Delbourgo, for getting behind this book, for her unwavering faith in me, and for being a true friend and mentor. I am forever grateful to my friend Christina Rossomando, who, for the third time in a row, has lent her generous spirit and discriminating ear to the writing of the book. Deep appreciation goes to Nicole Diamond for being this book's first champion. With great admiration and gratitude I thank my savvy and kind editor, Marcela Landres, for giving *Wish It* its sparkle and shine. Profound appreciation to Scott Idelman for dressing the book in its wonderful cover as well as Liz Bevilacqua for handling the book with care, Mark Gompertz, Chris Lloreda, Trish Todd, Marcia Burch, Francine Kass, Marcia Peterson, Martha Schwartz, Joy O'Meara, Jaime Putorti, Laurie Cotumaccio, London King, and everyone else at Simon & Schuster for their commitment and hard work. Big thank you to Fran Fisher for carefully reviewing the manuscript. Special thanks to Robin Blakely for her insights, creative spirit, steady support, and for helping to bring the principles of Life Integration to the surface. Additional gratitude to everyone at Livingston Communications for their help and commitment. For his patience, creativity, and skill I am indebted to Lee Roesner for shepherding my web site into the twenty-first century. Hats off to the guys at DLS Internet Services for keeping my web site up and running. Mary Ellen Blanchard continues to wield miraculous powers over my computer; without her constant help and support, I'd be writing longhand. Many thanks to the Fairygodmother Foundation for their support and good work.

I am most grateful to the people who spoke to me about their wishes and dreams, particularly those who provided that extra oomph at the eleventh hour. Appreciation also goes to ProfNet for helping me find the people who wish, dream, and do.

For their insights, steady encouragement, and friendship, many hundreds of thanks to Lisa Comegna, Joe Gemignani, Robin LaBorwit, Victoria Moran, Phyllis Wagner, Laura Zuckerman, Pat DeLuca, Judith Kalfon, Laura Levin, Evy Severino, Linda Muskin, Pam Bernstein, Valerie Gallin, Michele Pritzker, Lynne Caplan, Lori DeKalo, Sallyan Windt, Kelly James-Enger, Dorothy Foltz-Gray, Candy Spreckman, Cyndy Robin, Merle D'Alba, Jerry Flach, Marilyn Melia, Jeanie Rock, Donna Greenberg, Sharon Reichler, my sister Wendy Zevin, and my sister-in-law Sheri Levine. For their continued support I thank my mother, Elinor Zevin, my brother, Robert Zevin, and Evelyn Thomas. Warm thanks and eternal appreciation to Heidi Rosenberg for helping this rabbit become real.

I am, once again, immensely grateful to Jonathan Levine for enduring the months that I spent working on this book and for his steady love and encouragement.

Finally, infinite gratitude and from-here-to-eternity love to my children, Esther and Philip, who make my heart sing.

To accomplish great things
we must not only act but also dream
not only plan, but also believe.
　　　　　—Anatole France

Contents

Introduction

Welcome! You're about to embark upon an exciting journey that will help you define, pursue, and capture your dreams. In *Wish It, Dream It, Do It: Turn the Life You're Living into the Life You Want*, you will learn how to combine your dreams and wishes with practical strategies that will help you achieve what you really want from life. Maybe you'd like to run your own business or perhaps you've always wanted to paint in a private studio. Or you've put off teaching but have finally decided to obtain your certificate. You might simply want a change in your life and decide to relocate to another city.

The woman who follows her bliss doesn't simply gaze at the stars or daydream about becoming a millionaire. This dream catcher does something about what's missing in her life. And although she holds on to her dream like a hat on a cold, blustery day, she also engages in and embraces the hard, hard work that wishes and dreams require but rarely disclose. In other words, she will wish it, dream it, and, finally, do it.

In all fifty-two chapters—one for each week of the year—I provide a four-part strategy that will help you combine your inner resources with external sources of support, such as mentors, workshops, other books, colleagues, and friends and family. Each chapter will propel you to (1) ask, (2) experiment, (3) practice, and (4) affirm. This approach focuses on what's inside—what moves you, makes you happy, and drives you to become a whole and authentic individual. For example, in Listen to Your Quiet, you'll ask yourself questions such as, "What have I not been hearing?" and "Do my dreams have a voice that's loud enough to hear?" In the chapter Summon Your Creativity, you'll learn how to tap in to your personal well of creativity, test your problem-solving skills, and stretch your imagination. After reading Dress the Part before You Get the Part, you'll master the art of practicing to be what you want to become without waiting for the recognition and financial rewards that often accompany success. In all, you will learn how to turn the life you're living into the life you want.

Once you've completed the practice exercises you'll have your own set of instructions for creating a life that closely aligns with your physical, emotional, and spiritual needs. Also, I will encourage you to experiment with the what-ifs, so that you may get a sense of what might happen if, indeed, you try on your dreams. You'll learn how to test yourself without worrying about failing or being judged. The strategies for becoming a happier, more authentic you are set forth as experiments—ideas that you can test for usefulness and applicability to your own life. Once you've read about and absorbed the strategies, you'll put them into practice in a way that suits your life. Each chapter closes with an affirmation—a show of support and a few words intended to coax you toward taking the next step. Ultimately, you will learn how to create and then live by your affirmations.

As a workbook, Wish It, Dream It, Do It gives you an opportunity to look inside yourself to determine what you deem important. Like others, you've probably begun to realize that the bottom line means more than the ability to carry a heavy mortgage or buy the shiniest SUV. You may love your work but suffer an inexplicable void in your personal life. Indeed, your devotion to your job may impede your progress toward forming deep and lasting relationships outside of work. You may be the star performer in the office when the real stage is what you crave. On the other hand, perhaps you're surrounded by a loving family and supportive friends and enjoy a high standard of living. Yet, deep down you might feel unfulfilled and wonder what's missing from your life. Maybe you'd like to be more connected to your community and to volunteer your time to a special group. Perhaps you've always wanted to hike the Appalachian Trail but have never taken the time. The questions and assignments offered here will help you access the part of you that wants to break free of frustration and move forward. Whether you've just started your career or begun to hear a small voice inside that's itching for something more—a job that's more closely aligned with your values or a hobby that accommodates your special talents—*Wish It, Dream It, Do It* will gently accompany you on the most important path you'll ever take.

I offer you this book to support you on your journey. May its principles guide and inspire you to action to compose a truly fulfilling life.

~ week 1 ~

Take a Step

A journey of a thousand miles begins with a single step.

—Lao-tzu, Chinese proverb

ask

1. What did I wish for when I was young?
2. As a child, did my wishes and dreams ever come true?
3. Am I willing to wish, dream, and do, even though I'm not always sure what I'm wishing for?
4. Today, right now, am I paying attention to the parts of my life that matter the most?
5. What's the first thing I need to do before I embark upon this year-long journey?
6. Am I prepared for the hard work ahead?
7. What will my life look like in a year?

Like you, *Wish It, Dream It, Do It* is comprised of many interrelated pieces. What brings about movement in one part of your life is likely to promote activity in other areas as well. On the flip side, if you're stuck in one situation, another aspect of your life may come to a standstill, too. Applying the holistic principles set forth in *Wish It, Dream It, Do It* will enhance your ability to become whole and centered.

1

The material will help you uncover and reexamine old beliefs that have curtailed your efforts to wish, dream, and do. Some strategies will test your commitment and resolve to create the kind of life you've always wanted. Each week you'll learn how to master a new strategy, but more important, you'll learn something new about yourself. Throughout the book you'll find the support and encouragement you need to propel and maintain your progress.

As you immerse yourself in the strategies presented here, you will discover what you're meant to do, your purpose. But don't expect your heart's desire to remain constant as you work your way through the book. At one moment your dream will be in picture-perfect focus. Perhaps your dream to pursue a master's in social work is beginning to fit in nicely with your schedule and you're prepared to register for your first class. At the next moment, however, your dream might resemble a swirling blur preparing to become another image, different from the one that came before it but more defined, maybe even a little sharper—you still want the degree, but you're thinking that maybe you'd first like to get some experience in the field.

Throughout the process you will occasionally come face-to-face with certain fears. Many of us worry that others will find out that we're frauds. This is especially true when we begin to inch ever so slowly toward our dreams. Remember this: Pursuing your dreams is never a fraudulent act. Still, like little hooded goblins, these fears may linger longer than you'd like. You can try to shake free of their power, but they're stubborn and they'll hang on. If you want to capture your dreams, you must learn to coexist with these fears. Certainly, some of your fears will surrender. Others, though, will want to stick around. You can either allow those hangers-on to hold you back or face them head-on and say, "Fine!

You're not going to let go? Well, hold on, because it's going to be quite a ride."

experiment

Suspend your disbelief. Okay, so you've never found a four-leaf clover or thrown a penny into a wishing well. Perhaps you don't even think about the stars or notice when one shoots across the horizon in a blaze of glory. Well, before you even turn the page, relinquish your doubts—for at least a week—so that you will be more receptive to the possibilities and opportunities that life has in store.

Set your own pace. Ideally, you'll want to work your way through this book chapter by chapter. If you rush ahead you may neglect important questions and exercises intended to help you create the life you want. On the other hand, you know yourself best and should therefore be the judge of how quickly or slowly to take this journey. If you prefer to skip around and find what applies to where you are in life, by all means do what works for you.

Find a wish it partner or form a group. You may want to enhance your efforts by finding a partner who shares your desire to wish, dream, and do. A partner can be a good sounding board and share experiences as the two of you move along your journeys. A group effort can be effective as well, although you might want to consider a few ground rules before you begin. If you do join up with like-minded individuals, make sure everyone is in it for the right reason—mutual support. (Please see One More Thought, p. 267, for details on how to form a Wish It Group.)

Celebrate every achievement—small and large. Don't let your achievements slip by unnoticed. Celebrate whenever you can. Pick up your favorite carry-out and eat by candlelight one night. Send yourself a congratulations card. Use a certificate template on your computer and print out your personal award. Recognizing and honoring each success—major and minor—is the best affirmation you can give yourself.

practice

How would I like my life to look in a year?

1. _____

_____

2. _____

_____

3. _____

_____

The first steps I can take to wish, dream, and do include:

1. _____

_____

2. _____

_____

3. _____

_____

What are the initial challenges I'm likely to encounter?

1. _____

_____

2. _____

_____

3. _____

_____

affirm

As I take a step to wish, dream, and do, I imagine an entire galaxy of infinite hope.

As I take a step, I

_____

_____

~ week 2 ~

Summon Your Creativity

Many people are inventive, sometimes cleverly so. But real creativity begins with the drive to work on and on and on.
—Margueritte Harmon Bro, *Sarah* (1949)

ask

1. Do I consider myself creative?
2. Do I admire other people's creativity?
3. Do I ever get stuck, unable to create anything?
4. How can my negative and positive self-perceptions coexist so that I don't get stuck?
5. How can I respond to my critical self-talk?
6. Do I have enough time and quiet to express my creativity?
7. What inspires me?

Sometimes creativity is revealed not through one's artistic flair but more in an individual's ability to withstand adversity. Creative budgeting allows the family whose dual income is suddenly cut in half by a layoff to maintain a roof over their heads and keep their kids clothed and fed. The event planner who must suddenly change a meeting venue relies on a clear mind and creativity to avert a crisis. Creativity also serves as an outlet for tension. When my son and I are in a tug-of-war over important issues like tying his shoes or drinking his milk, I dip into my creative reservoir and come up with something that softens the strain and leads us to some form of resolution ("You drink half your milk and I'll put the candy back in your lunchbox").

As you work hard to turn your wishes and dreams into reality, try dipping into your well of creativity. Perhaps you're a creative connector, someone who's good at hooking people together for a common good. Many years ago my mother decided that a busy intersection near our home needed a traffic light; accidents there were a common occurrence. Fed up, she put her networking skills to use. She pulled together key individuals from various groups (i.e., transportation, law enforcement, citizenry), which was an essential strategy toward garnering support, and ultimately achieved her goal. Remember, too, that your creative drive—your potential to imagine something new and different—isn't necessarily defined by your ability to paint or act or sing. Phyllis, a Mary Kay consultant, applies her artistic background to packaging each product she sells with a memorable, artistic flair. Adorned with festive ribbon and other decorative accoutrements, each item she sells has her signature appearance. Phyllis takes enormous pleasure in preparing the orders (and often it takes hours!), yet she knows that packaging is an integral part of successful selling.

Apple founder Steve Jobs once said that the Macintosh flourished because the team members working on it were historians, poets, musicians, and artists who coincidentally were excellent computer scientists as well. This confluence of art and science can be found everywhere from awe-inspiring suspension bridges to the stark silhouette of a leafless tree in the middle of winter.

Contrary to what you may have heard or said in the past—"I

don't have a creative bone in my body!"—creativity can be cultivated, drawn out (so to speak), and nurtured. But don't expect
your imagination to burst forth without assistance. You need to
give breath to your creative soul. Only then will it begin to show
some life of its own.

Denying your creative spirit, especially as you race toward com-
pleting your goals, is easy to do but no less destructive. Whenever
you rush a process—particularly a creative one—you risk missing
a fundamental component, one that could move you closer to your
dream. You may not hear an important point of view, or you might
overlook a helpful article buried on a page deep inside your daily
newspaper. Tending to your creative soul takes time. So remember
to slow down and pay attention.

experiment

Write a creativity mission statement. One of the best ways to
catch a glimpse of your just-maybe-it-might-happen future is to
write about it. Your creativity mission statement should reflect not
only your desires but the values you attach to the process. It can be
as long as several pages or as short as a few words. For example,
you might write, "I will live each day with the courage to incorporate my creative instincts whenever possible." Be prepared to evaluate and update this on a regular basis. Add a favorite quotation at
the end for extra encouragement. Make copies and keep them
handy—in your glove compartment, on the fridge, on your computer—anywhere you spend a lot of time.

Take a class. Five years ago, Joanie, an artist and mother of three,
enrolled in two portrait-painting classes. Every Tuesday and

Thursday (barring a sick kid or other emergency), Joanie carried her supplies up five flights of stairs to the top of a mansion that now houses classrooms. "I always felt I could be a good painter," she says. "And if I could paint a person then I'd feel as if I were meeting a big challenge." While the classes provided an outlet for her skills and talent, the work was hard and a constant struggle. "Usually, I felt as if I were walking into a wrestling match. Sometimes I was the one who was pinned down. Afterward, I'd leave the class exhausted." Still, Joanie reports that she knows she accomplished something when she entered that zone in which the work became effortless. She also derived inspiration from her classmates. "One woman was ninety," she says. "I was like the youngster with years to go. That gave me a lot of encouragement and hope." Today, Joanie paints in her own studio not far from her home.

Make a collage. When I finally got serious about creating my first web site I relied on my own skills for some of the artwork. As a writer, I draw so much of my work from what I've observed, what others have done on my behalf, and how people have influenced me. I decided the best way to portray myself would be through a collage. I began collecting bits and pieces of my life that could be copied, reduced, glued down, and finally scanned into the twenty-first century—a letter my father wrote to his parents from Guam during World War II, a seaside image painted by my daughter, the canceled postage on an envelope containing a meaningful letter. The exercise took weeks to complete, but the outcome is a constant reminder of what's important in my life. Your collage doesn't need to go on the Internet; you could frame it for your bathroom or keep it in a drawer under lock and key. It is the process of collecting images that is important. In order to turn what you want into what is yours, you need to wake up what may be dormant. Dig through photographs, clip images from a variety of magazines, and leaf through catalogs as you explore and collect the pieces that reflect not only who you are but who you are going to become.

practice

People used to tell me I was creative because I could:

1. _____

_____

2. _____

_____

3. _____

_____

I used to bury my creative interests by:

1. _____

_____

2. _____

_____

3. _____

_____

Even if I stumble and make mistakes, my creative soul matters because:

1. _____

_____

2. _____

_____

3. _____

_____

affirm

Cultivating my creativity will bring clarity to the murky parts of my life and movement to what's been standing still.

Cultivating my creativity will

_____

_____

~ week 3 ~

Put It in Writing

*Recording happiness made it last longer, we felt,
and recording sorrow dramatized it and took away
its bitterness; and often we settled some problem
which beset us even while we wrote about it.*
—Dorothy Day, *From Union Square to Rome*
(1940)

ask

1. Am I reluctant to put my wishes and dreams in writing? Why?
2. How can I express in written words what I can't always say out loud?
3. What about privacy? Can I trust others not to read my private thoughts?
4. Do I need any special skills to put my thoughts on paper?
5. Am I willing to take the time necessary to put my dreams onto paper?
6. What could I reasonably expect to write given my busy schedule?
7. Will writing down my goals really make them happen?

When we put our wishes and dreams on paper we amplify and validate our innermost heart's desire. As kids we turned to our dear diaries, sometimes under lock and key—our private sounding boards that neither judged nor disapproved. As adults, we reach for our journals to record and make sense of our days.

By putting it in writing, you literally give yourself a mind sweep, a clearing away of worry, self-doubt, inner-critic talk, and vexing chatter. You thereby make room for the creative doer who wants desperately to step out of the noise and into a space where the hard work can begin.

Putting it in writing allows you to track your progress as well. For example, Kelly James-Enger, an author and freelance writer, always documents her goals. "I write them down and keep them posted by my computer where I can see them all day," she says. "I think that's really helped me to reach my goals because they're always right in front of me, a real reminder of what I'm trying to accomplish."

Keeping a journal can help, too; it's like having a calendar of thoughts, ideas, and feelings. You don't have to write every day and you certainly don't need to review everything you've written. But it's useful sometimes to turn back and read with some perspective what came tumbling out of your consciousness earlier. It's as if you're giving the experience two lives—the one you lived and the one in review. It is in that space—between the two—that change occurs.

Many of us live by to-do lists, whether they're recorded on a handheld computer or a yellow Post-it stuck on the refrigerator. But how often do we list our dreams? My to-do list usually looks like this:

1. Eggs
2. Bread
3. Call school

4. Return library books
5. Go to post office
6. Write thank-yous
7. Bank

What does your list look like? Is it filled with action items that accommodate other people? Does it accommodate your heart's desire?

What if you could include your wishes and dreams on your to-do list? What if you kept a separate inventory, not of what you need to pick up at the grocery store or drop off at the cleaners but of what brought you the widest grin and the fullest heart? What if putting it in writing really could make it happen? Well, you'd probably start right now. In fact, before you read another word, grab a piece of paper. Anything will do. You can even jot things down in the margins of this page. So, go ahead and write your wish list. Try to avoid things like home furnishings, clothes, and jewelry. Instead, consider what will bring you unfettered joy and happiness or some peace—a respite from your busy schedule. That could mean a couple hours a week with a personal trainer, a session or two with a professional organizer, or a monthly dinner with your inner circle of friends. Remember that we're talking about your heart's desire here, not your need for *stuff*.

Once you begin to put your wishes and dreams in writing, your words take on immense power. Your words—whether they're written on scraps of paper or organized into files on your computer—become tools that help you calibrate, repair, and build your dreams. That you do nothing with your words once they're released onto the page doesn't minimize their importance. Think of your writing as a form of prayer—a release of the dialogue between your head and your heart.

experiment

Keep a folder. A manila folder works wonders. It's low tech, cheap, and offers plenty of blank space to jot down even more thoughts. Keep a folder or several—in your kitchen, in the top drawer of your desk at work, anywhere—handy so that you'll have a safe place for all your wonderful ideas. More than anything your folder is a symbol of your commitment to wish, dream, and do. It's a tangible reminder that your dreams are worthy of safekeeping.

Practice "anywhere anytime" writing. You don't have to be sitting at a desk or reclining in a chair to write down your wishes and dreams. You don't even have to be in the mood to write. You just need to *do* it. I made the mistake once of leaving extra paper at home when my family and I visited an exhibit at Chicago's wonderful Art Institute. I had to borrow a pen from a guard and jot down some thoughts on my check register. My words were barely legible, but it was better than relying on my memory. Putting it in writing a few minutes in the morning, in the middle of the day, or just before you go to sleep at night will eventually translate into something that looks a lot like progress.

Journal. Record your wishes and dreams (and what you're doing about them) in a journal. An inexpensive spiral notebook is fine, though you might want to treat yourself to something with a little more pizzazz. My journal pages include my notations plus wonderful printed quotations that guide and inspire me. Think of your journal as your private repository for the whirlwind that circulates within your mind. If you're worried that someone will pry, make it clear that your journal belongs to you and you expect others to respect your privacy. You make the rules when it comes to reading your entries. You can review every month or disregard them altogether. The idea is to empty your head onto the blank page.

Send yourself status reports. A status report is a good indicator of how things are progressing. At the end of each month, take a few minutes to evaluate your progress. You don't even have to write full sentences. Just the facts. My report may look something like: "Web site almost complete, invitation list set, office still needs organizing, outline chapters of next book . . ."

practice

I've always wanted to express my feelings about:

1. _____

   _____

2. _____

   _____

3. _____

   _____

If I could make three wishes, they'd be:

1. _____

   _____

2. _____

   _____

3. _____

_____

I'm willing to create a ritual of writing by:

1. _____

_____

2. _____

_____

3. _____

_____

affirm

Putting my wishes and dreams in writing is one way of preserving them and ensuring their continued inspiration.

Putting my wishes and dreams in writing will

_____

_____

~ week 4 ~

Dress the Part Before You Get the Part

The longer you wear pearls, the realer they become.
—Colette, *Cheri* (1920)

ask

1. Do I talk about my dreams with assuredness and hope?
2. Can I smile when I really would rather not?
3. Am I worried that I might be perceived as a fraud?
4. Can I act "as if" and be scared at the same time?
5. Do I have the tools I need to practice for the part?
6. Does my image project what I want people to see?
7. What if I never get the part?

Sometimes we deny ourselves an opportunity simply because we don't think we fit the part. We might fail. Worse, we might even succeed—and then what? Perhaps your parents wanted to protect you from disappointment and in the process held you back from taking risks. Perhaps you wanted to try out for the school play and you were led to believe that no one like you ever got the part, so why bother. Maybe you were discouraged from pursuing a sport because "you might get hurt" or were told you weren't smart enough for the debate team. This is a terribly depressing way to look at the world and is particularly disheartening if you've got even the smallest pinch of pixie dust with which to dream. This is why you must dress the part before you get the part.

This isn't about pretending to be someone you're not or tempting fate by placing yourself in another person's shoes. It's about training for the role you're pursuing. It's as if you are the producer, director, and star of your vision. Too often, though, when we start fantasizing about that moment we say things like, "That would be too good to be true," "It'll never happen," and, "Who am I kidding?" But those are old lines that need rewriting. A new script might include phrases like, "I can do this," "I am meant to do this," and, "This is what I've always wanted."

Disarming the negative and replacing it with something positive is often just a matter of perception. If you decide, for instance, that you're beautiful, then you'll probably carry yourself with more grace and pride. In the same way, if you can dress the part before you get the part, you will move closer toward turning what you want into what is yours.

Unfortunately, we're not always given the tools we need to get started. You may have heard someone say, "Go for your dreams! You can be whatever you want to be!" *Okay. How do I do that?* You need to act "as if"—as if you've already got the job, the part, the money, the success, the satisfaction. Jacqueline Jurica, owner of Jacqueline's of Northbrook, acted "as if" from the moment she decided to enter the jewelry business. Unlike many of her peers today, Jacqueline did not begin her career in a family-owned business. "I started working with jewelry when I was fifteen," she says. "I didn't have an established clientele or a foundation upon which to build. Walking into a family-run store would've been much easier, but I had a vision of opening my own stores one day, so instead of dwelling on what I didn't have, I focused on my dream. I slowly began to gain the customers' trust and confidence and now, years later, I own two thriving jewelry stores. Most important, though, are the strong relationships I've developed with my customers over the years since I first started working." Like Jacqueline, the more you dress the part, the better you become at visualizing your dream. More important, you train others to see you in the same way.

experiment

Learn your lines. Maybe you've dreamed of leaving a high-powered finance position to become a teacher. Your family has doubts about your decision and your colleagues shake their heads, wondering out loud how you'll survive. Put their doubts (and your own) to rest by trying the part on for size. Instead of sleeping in, get up early on a Saturday morning and log on to www.nea.org, the official web site for the National Education Association. Or go to any number of sources that focus on teaching. Learn the language and absorb the issues.

Research your role. If you want to become a writer, subscribe to a few online writing magazines and check out the print publications at the library and the bookstore. Buy stationery that features a writing motif. Read autobiographies and biographies about writers. You'll probably learn that there were times in their careers when they wanted to quit or never thought they'd get to where they ended up.

Imitate the best. When you encounter someone who's doing what you'd like to do, watch and listen carefully. Why is she successful? How does she move through a typical day? Get to know the people you emulate. Ask them how they got started and about the obstacles they encountered along the way. Take notes if necessary. If they're especially generous with their time and expertise, send a thank-you note.

Rehearse. How would you act on the first day of your dream job? If you received an award, what would you say in your acceptance speech? As your dreams come true—and they will—you'll be glad you took the time to prepare. Rehearse in your car, in the shower, anywhere. You may be surprised at how well you know your lines.

practice

I've always admired and even wanted to be a little like:

1. _____

_____

2. _____

_____

3. _____

_____

The characteristics I most admire about this person are:

1. _____

_____

2. _____

_____

3. _____

_____

In order to act as if I've already won the part, I can alter my environment by:

1. _____

_____

2. _____

_____

3. _____

_____

affirm

When I dress the part before I get the part, my potential is in motion and clasps a piece of possibility.

When I dress the part before I get the part,

_____

_____

Embrace Your Imperfections

My instinct has always been to turn drawbacks into drawing cards.
—Marie Dressler, *The Life Story of an Ugly Duckling* (1924)

ask

1. What do I see when I look in the mirror?
2. When I'm talking to myself, do I use kind language or are my words critical and mean-spirited?
3. Can I get through an entire day without putting myself down either to myself or to others?
4. Do I constantly criticize my appearance?
5. How willing am I to actually embrace my imperfections?
6. Do I expect others to be perfect?
7. Is perfection really a goal anyway?

Nobody's perfect. We say it all the time—when a friend laments her poor judgment, when a child spills a glass of milk, or whenever we fall short of our own expectations. Still, perfection seems to be something to shoot for, a goal, a magical, if-only-we-could-get-there destination. Perfection is especially tempting when we're wishing, dreaming, and doing. It's as if we equate perfection with accomplishment. But if that's true, how could so many innovations be the result of countless mistakes and accidents? Think Post-its and penicillin.

As you work to turn what you want into what is yours, strive to recognize that there is no such thing as a perfect person. Therefore, your goal should not be to become the *best* but the *best you can be.* The difference lies in your ability to focus on your strengths, not someone else's. Think of it this way: The nuts and bolts you need from the hardware store should be perfect; your hair, on the other hand, probably has a mind of its own and will look fine despite your protests that it's much too something—long, short, straight, curly. A surgeon has no room for error when it comes to performing a procedure on your eye; but the first draft of your business plan will probably need work.

Embrace and celebrate your imperfections. They're what make you *you*, separating you from the pack. Remember that this whole love affair with perfection usually has something to do with others. Some people are simply programmed to find fault with everything, including you. But that's their thing, and doesn't have to be yours. As you begin to consider the whole package—your gifts and your faults—try to focus more on all the good things you do, not on what you have or how you look. So your skin may not be perfectly clear and that M.F.A. you've always dreamed of still belongs to someone else. You can still find true love or write a great novel.

This week, applaud your imperfections. Say "bravo" to what makes you special and sets you apart from everyone else. Consider, as well, what life might be like if you *were* perfect. What would you strive for? What would you want to know? Would life be nearly as interesting as it is now? How would you ever grow and change? What would you wish and dream for?

experiment

Do your best, not someone else's best. Most of us had parents and teachers, even bosses, who told us to do our best, and we did. But what did it mean? Whose "best" were we doing anyway? Do your own best, not your friend's or your colleague's. Admiring and trying to emulate someone else's success can be motivating. It becomes destructive and counterproductive, however, when your admiration jeopardizes your authenticity. You will never be just like anyone else—then again, no one else can be just like you, either.

Stop waiting. In many ways, perfectionism is the ultimate stumbling block to our progress. We wait until we can get it just right or until the time is perfect. The absence of perfect conditions becomes an excuse for not doing what we've set out to do. Instead of wishing, dreaming, and doing, we wait and procrastinate. Rather than seize opportunities to achieve, you look for reasons to stay inactive. Admit the shortcoming and change your mind-set. It's never too late to find your groove. For example, instead of waiting until you have enough money to go back to school to become a reading specialist or a certified financial planner, continue saving and begin your instruction immediately. Read whatever you can and conduct informational interviews with people working in the field. Just because you haven't arrived doesn't mean that you're not going to reach your destination.

Don't invite failure. Striving for perfection will inevitably bring you face-to-face with failure. Eventually, the fear of and discomfort with defeat are enough to stop your efforts altogether.

Challenges become insurmountable obstacles of open-ended possibilities. If you have a history of setting yourself up for failure, consider sidestepping perfection. Think of your flaws as stepping-stones toward success.

Take baby steps. If embracing your imperfections is overwhelming, take small steps. Give yourself a break by softening the language you use to describe yourself. Promise yourself a compliment once a day. Look in the mirror and smile at your beautiful face. Send yourself an encouraging greeting card. You'll laugh as you seal the envelope and chuckle again when it arrives in the mail a few days later.

practice

Sometimes I put off doing things because I'm waiting for:

1. _____

_____

2. _____

_____

3. _____

_____

I'm willing to be good enough at:

1. _____

_____

2. _____

_____

3. _____

_____

Once I accept my imperfections, I can:

1. _____

_____

2. _____

_____

3. _____

_____

affirm

Instead of expending energy on what I can't change or be, I pursue opportunities for growth, change, and happiness.

When I embrace my imperfections, I

_____

_____

~ week 6 ~

Show the World Who You Are

*Let's dare to be ourselves, for we do that bet-
ter than anyone else can.*
   —Sue Patton Thoele, *The Courage to Be Yourself*
                    (1988)

ask

1. How do others see me?
2. Do I ever let others define who I am?
3. What are my strengths? Weaknesses?
4. Can I differentiate between the person I am and the person I want to become?
5. Do I sometimes lose myself, forgetting my true self?
6. How important is it for me to conduct periodic self-assessments?
7. Do I respect myself?

Soon after my daughter entered junior high school, she completed an unusual assignment. "Mom, we need to bring ourselves in a bag." *Huh?* "We need to put stuff into a bag that says who we are." Ah, then I understood. It didn't take long for her to gather up the items—a family portrait, a test she had aced, pictures of friends, a notebook full of her own poetry. The homework assignment revealed as much about what she thought of herself as how she wanted others to see her. And it gave her an uncommon opportunity to look inward and consider what truly matters in her young and busy life. "One kid brought his baby sister last year, Mom." I got the picture.

We're constantly defined by who we are in relation to the people and events surrounding our lives. I'm a daughter, a mother, a wife, a sister, and a friend. Can all these roles peacefully coexist or do they split my soul apart, causing me to forget who I am? Before you can possibly move toward your dreams, you must move toward yourself. Become curious about your likes and dislikes. Ask yourself where you stand on certain issues. Recognize your breaking points, and take a sweeping view of all the pieces that compose your life.

You will embark on many journeys as you work toward turning the life you're living into the life you want. The most critical journey is the one that leads you inward. If you don't know who you are, your ability to make decisions—the ones that move you from wishing and dreaming to doing—will be thwarted again and again. Sometimes, when I'm questioning what I've done in my life and why I'm not further along, I ask myself about the preceding years and how that time contributed to the person I am today. For example, I couldn't have written this book ten years ago because I hadn't met the people who inspired me to wish, dream, and do. I had not yet accumulated the perspective, knowledge, and insight that I gained during those years.

Knowing who you are also is an important step toward *respecting* who you are. As you work hard to achieve your goals you will, undoubtedly, confront naysayers and doubters. The voices will come from family, friends, and people you hardly know. Some will be well intentioned; others may be malevolent and mean-spirited. You might be asked a lot of questions, too: "Are you sure that's what you want?"; "What about your job?"; "Why would you give up what you've worked so hard for?" Your patience and compassion—or resentment and anxiety—won't change others' opinions of you. But if you can easily access your self-respect, you'll know how to absorb and manage other people's points of view. Rather than dwell on what someone else said about you and your dreams, focus on what makes you a competent individual, a person of many talents, and a human being who won't back down and capitulate.

experiment

Bring yourself in a bag. You don't have to be in junior high to benefit from this exercise. Simply take a paper bag (or a canvas bag or even your favorite purse) and fill it with the things that are symbolic of who you are. You could even have a Bring Yourself in a Bag party. Enclose a lunch-sized brown paper bag in each invitation along with some instructions. At the party, set aside some time for everyone to introduce themselves. Watch the faces of your guests, too, as they pull out the items that compose their lives.

Write the résumé for the life you dream of. Consider your previous experience including paying jobs, volunteer positions, and any academic roles, such as class president or member of the cross-country team. Focus on the experiences that brought you the most satisfaction and joy. Go back as far as you like. For instance, if you took part in a community service project in high school, include that in your résumé. Then string these events together and look carefully for any patterns. You might discover something about your style that can be incorporated into your Wish It, Dream It, Do It plan. Ask yourself:

* What did I do?
* What did I enjoy?
* What turned me off?
* What did I learn?
* What did I achieve?
* What did others say about me?

Compose your epitaph. Asking yourself how you want to be remembered can be instructive and illuminating. It's one of those questions that can stop you cold, but it's not intended to halt your hard work or diminish your big dreams. It's a method to further understand yourself and recognize, rather quickly, what's really important in your life. Asking this question helps us bring value to who we are, which in turn makes us more self-aware. It also quickly puts our wishes and dreams into perspective.

practice

I want to know who I am because:

1. _____

_____

2. _____

_____

3. _____

_____

Sometimes I'm afraid to discover who I am because:

1. _____

_____

2. _____

_____

3. _____

_____

Here are the parts of myself that I'd like to change:

1. _____

_____

2. _____

_____

3. _____

_____

affirm

Instead of projecting an image of what others may expect to see, I reflect only what is real and true about me.

When I show myself to the world, I

_____

_____

Preserve and Manage Your Time

Alas! There is no casting anchor in the stream of time!

—Countess of Blessington,
Country Quarters, Vol. I (1850)

ask

1. How much time do I devote to pursuing my dreams?
2. Do I put things off? Why?
3. Do I ever miscalculate the time it takes for me to accomplish certain tasks?
4. Do I say "yes" too often when people ask for my time?
5. How would I fill an extra hour in the day?
6. Do I consider my free time sacred?
7. How would I feel if I could spend more time pursuing my dreams?

Most of us know that practicing effective time-management strategies can lead to a more productive and less stressful life. This is especially the case when we truly begin to value our time. Yet even after we've mastered the whole time-management thing we often neglect the moment—even ourselves—because we're so drawn to the tasks on our "what's next" lists. It's as if living on a schedule and being present are mutually exclusive. Unless we preserve our time—even become a little greedy with our time—the moments we need to wish, dream, and do will disappear without a trace.

Preparing for the unexpected is another strategy you'll want to master, since very often our wishes and dreams depend on opportunities that quite literally fall into our laps. For example, an unexpected call from a former colleague changed Linda's life in ways she could never have imagined. "A woman I had shared an office with started a public relations company with someone she met at a subsequent job. One day, out of the blue, my former officemate called and asked if I'd be interested in joining them. It was a risk and I had to make some significant changes, but it was the right thing at just the right time in my life," she says.

If you're overloaded to the extent that you can't accommodate an unplanned occurrence, the opportunity is quickly lost. Like Linda, you need to shift things around and become flexible in an instant. You can plan and plot for a lifetime, but ultimately time has its own schedule.

Evaluating your relationship with time will *take time.* You must truthfully assess how much time you currently devote to various aspects of your life—your self, your family, your work, your friends, your wishes and dreams. Don't rush this part. It is absolutely essential.

Sometimes we get entangled with time because we don't know what to do with it or we have so much to do; indeed, we may not even know where to begin. But is that really the case? Do we feel threatened by time? What if we use up a certain amount of time and can't show anything for our efforts? What if we discover something about ourselves and feel compelled to change, which could shift the amount of time we need? Time is risky. But then so are dreams. As you work to create your time-management system—one that allows you to preserve the moments you need to wish, dream, and do—take a few risks and try out new strategies. Schedule lunch with your spouse or partner. Make a date with your child. Block out personal time for yourself, too. Give these "appointments" high priority by jotting them on your calendar, computer, or PDA. If you don't devote enough time to your friends and loved ones, your relationships will suffer, which will adversely affect your ability to turn what you want into what is yours. As hard as you might try to separate work from family and friends, the reality is that these disparate elements of your life are really quite connected. Once you begin to integrate these pieces—weave them into a tapestry—you will find that the whole really is larger than the sum of its parts. For example, if you spend time with your child—even fifteen minutes on the couch watching television together—she'll be more secure in her relationship with you. If your child is relatively secure, chances are she'll cooperate in a way that gives you more freedom—to get a little extra work done on the computer, finish up a phone call, or simply organize your desk at the end of the day. When your work life suffers, your personal life is adversely affected as well, and vice versa. Instead of relegating people to the fringes of your schedule, preserve your time with them. The moments themselves might be short-lived, but the relationships can last a lifetime.

experiment

Ask three questions. Sometimes when I'm shopping and see a must-have, I ask myself three questions: (1) Do I want it? (2) How much will it cost? and (3) Can I afford it? You can do the same with your time. If something comes up or if you're questioning the necessity of doing a particular task, ask yourself: (1) Do I want/need to do this? (2) How much time will it take? and (3) Can I afford the time? Once you begin dissecting your tasks in this way, you'll be able to determine more clearly and with greater resolve what you really do have time for in your twenty-four-hour day.

Schedule play as well as work. If you're always working and leave little time for play or idleness, you lose perspective. Work becomes all-consuming, an addiction. Addictions rarely accommodate a clear and truthful path for creativity, the juice of your wishes and dreams. Without worrying about the consequences, infuse one or more of your days this week with something other than work. That includes any responsibilities at home, too. It doesn't matter how you spend it or what you call it. What matters is that you make those times as important as the business meetings and doctors' appointments that appear on your daily planner.

Manage your time-management system. If your time-management system is driving you nuts, change it. If you're not charged up by the latest techno gadget or can't stand the thought of dealing with a page-a-day calendar, step back and reexamine your needs. I cut loose from a paper planner and dived right into the PDA trend, only to find that I missed my old way of managing time. I'm back to my traditional planner, though I do use the PDA to keep track of all my contacts.

Be on time. Do you suffer from chronic lateness? Are you always rushing to get out the door? Do you have a reputation for never being on time? If you answered "yes" to just one of these questions, you need to examine exactly why you can't be on time. It's taken me years! But I think I finally figured it out. My epiphany occurred when my husband finally said in exasperation one Saturday, "Stop trying to cram every single thing into one day!" Is that what I was doing? Apparently. By taking an honest look at what you can reasonably expect to complete in one day, you're likely to work smarter, get things done more easily, and be on time, especially when others are depending on you.

practice

Currently, I preserve and manage my time by:

1. _____

_____

2. _____

_____

3. _____

_____

I probably spend too much time doing:

1. _____

_____

2. _____

_____

3. _____

_____

I can more easily turn the life I'm living into the life I want if I spend more time doing:

1. _____

   _____

2. _____

   _____

3. _____

   _____

affirm

Rather than sneak around time or fill it unwisely, I commit to a schedule that promotes organization, reduces stress, and preserves a part of myself.

When I preserve and manage my time, I

_____

_____

Cross Train

Experience is what you get looking for some-thing else.
—Mary Pettibone Pool, *A Glass Eye at a Keyhole*
(1938)

ask

1. Am I willing to participate in activities at which I might not excel?
2. What prevents me from stepping outside my zone of comfort?
3. Is it hard for me to break away from my work in·order to pursue something unrelated to it?
4. How can I expand my knowledge of unfamiliar, but interesting, topics?
5. Whom do I personally know who's well rounded?
6. Whom do I admire—from afar—for her Renaissance persona?
7. What are some things I've always wanted to do?

Cross training challenges your body to perform at its best while giving your muscles the time they need to rest and recover. You can do the same for your emotional and psychological health by apply-ing these principles to the way in which you embrace the world around you. It is tempting and sometimes absolutely essential to focus exclusively on your dreams. Yet, when concentrating on just one subject we risk losing the grand perspective, missing out on serendipitous discoveries and short-changing our potential. We also move further and further from living an integrated life, one that encompasses more than what we can possibly imagine.

For Jennifer Popple, cross training moves far beyond her role as a fitness expert. "I have the luxury of hiking, spinning, kayaking, and practicing yoga on a regular basis," she says. "But it's that interest in learning new things and constantly challenging myself that helps me create balance within all aspects of my life." Jennifer's thirst for knowledge is often accompanied by a sense of accomplishment, whether she's mastered a new sport or traveled to another country. In addition to feeling fulfilled and joyful, Jennifer is open to new kinds of thinking and therefore can relate more effectively with a variety of people. This skill alone helps Jennifer successfully wish, dream, and do. Rather than be deterred by something that's unfamiliar—and uncomfortable—Jennifer welcomes changes and differences. Indeed, she seeks variety in life.

By cross training in your daily life you build new skills—intellectual, social, and physical. In the process your capacity to understand expands, which leads to more tolerance of other points of view. Too often we dismiss new ideas simply because they are unfamiliar and untested. Instead of walking away from what you don't know or standing for too long in one place, consider the beauty of something undiscovered. Often it's what we haven't tried that turns into our most fulfilling life experiences. Once, when a new guest arrived at Lake Austin Spa Resort, program director Robbie Hudson faced an unprecedented challenge. "Mary had signed up for a package that included one fifty-minute personal consultation or training," says

Robbie. "But Mary decided that she didn't want to book a training because she was already working with a personal trainer at home on a regular basis. I gently suggested that maybe she'd want to take advantage of all the options we offered, and that she try sculling on the waters of Lake Austin. She said there'd really be no point since she didn't live near water where she could try this at home.

"As it turns out, Mary returned the next morning and said that she'd try sculling after all. She had a good time—was a quick learner and seemed to enjoy herself. One week later I received a handwritten letter from her telling me she'd loved the sculling lesson, which turned out to be a life-changing experience. She'd enjoyed the physical and mental challenge of focus and concentration and the spiritual connection to nature, and contrary to what she'd said earlier, would make an effort to seek out a place near her home where she might scull again."

experiment

Don't get too comfortable. Routine and familiarity can soothe, comfort, and reduce stress. Too much of the same thing can also breed boredom, restlessness, and dissatisfaction. It's best to scramble up your patterns once in a while. Attend a networking meeting in the next town over. Study the marketing efforts of someone in an entirely different kind of business. Read a novel instead of a self-help book (reverse that if you usually read fiction). Listen to National Public Radio as well as your local news.

Pick three. Pick three things you've wanted to do that will lift you out of your normal routine. I live in a suburb of one of the best cities in America; yet I rarely make it to town. But I'm starting to change that by

committing to infrequent though regularly scheduled forays into the city. I'm never sure what new discovery will be waiting at an exhibit, on a menu, or even on the street. So far, I've spotted bovine beauties ("Cows on Parade") and dozens of fiberglass chairs, sofas, TVs, and ottomans decorated by local artists ("Suite Home Chicago").

Take an elective. Go back to school to study art, photography, music, or drama. Even if your current focus is as far away from art as you can imagine, consider a workshop—or even a two-hour visit to your local art gallery—that will introduce you to new principles and philosophies. Dario Nardi, an assistant math professor at UCLA, believes that cross training helps us hone our learning skills. "When we expose ourselves to different areas of study we learn how to learn with more open and discriminating minds." Dario, who also surfs and plays guitar, brings his penchant for cross training into the classroom as well. "I suspect that my varied background—life experience and education—gives me more personality and more flexible boundaries with people as well as a tendency to assign homework that is not the usual fare students are generally forced to digest."

practice

I have always wanted to try to do the following:

1. _____

   _____

2. _____

   _____

3. _____

   _____

In the next six weeks, I will rent a movie, borrow a book, and read a magazine article on at least two of the following subjects:

1. _____

   _____

2. _____

   _____

3. _____

   _____

When I step outside my comfort zone in order to learn something new, I feel:

1. _____

   _____

2. _____

   _____

3. _____

   _____

affirm

When I cross train and add diversity to my life, I open myself up to unseen, yet promising, opportunities.

When I cross train and add diversity to my life, I

_____

_____

~ week 9 ~

Be (a Little) Courageous

How cool, how quiet is true courage!
—Fanny Burney, *Evelina* (1778)

ask

1. If I could eliminate one fear, what would that be?
2. Whom do I admire for her courage?
3. What makes me courageous?
4. Am I my own best advocate?
5. What happens in my life when my courage is hard to find?
6. What happens in my life when my courage is front and center?
7. Am I willing to feel the anxiety that may accompany acts of courage?

We are inspired and awed by highly trained people who overcome huge odds to save lives and help make the world a better place. But being brave can be mundane as well. Certainly, some situations call for more bravery than others do. Living with and managing an illness takes tremendous fortitude. Soothing an angry customer calls for patience and diplomacy and sometimes even courage. Both demand resources that can come only from within. But you can't tap in to those resources if they're not there. That's why we all need to have courage, the kind that sits tight and waits patiently for when we need it most *and* the kind that walks beside us wherever we go.

In many ways, courage is faith wearing heavy boots, ready for inclement weather and prepared to face just about anything. Sometimes courage has a mind of its own, too, and marches forward despite our protests and without our approval. Instead of being a stranger, our courage becomes our faith standing guard. Sometimes your courage might take you to places that you'd never take yourself. Of course, some fears are good for us. They tell us when danger is near and often prevent us from harm and injury. But some fears can erode our tenacity and boldness and cause us to give up.

Remember this about bravery: Standing up for someone else, particularly someone you love, is generally a lot easier than doing so for yourself. I'd stand in front of a truck before I'd allow my children to get hurt. But do I have the same instincts when it comes to my own life? More important, would you display as much courage for your own life?

Our wishes and dreams fare so much better when we have a little courage—courage to stand up for our beliefs, courage to face the unknown, courage to be successful. When you wish, dream, and do, a successful outcome is directly related to your willingness to take a risk. Assaf Tarnopolsky, cofounder of the West Coast Crepe King, has always associated risk with plain old tenacity. "When you fall down, you get right back up," he says. "We've sweated and encountered some setbacks that are part of any start-up, but I always remind myself that we've got a great concept and an incredible product. Without taking risks, success would be out of reach instead of around the corner."

Still, risk can produce so much anxiety that you begin to wonder why you're pursuing a passion in the first place. Yet, demonstrating a brave point of view can help you wind through the morass of the unknown, self-doubt, and fear. You won't always be able to explain your courage—to others or to yourself. After overcoming a significant hurdle, for example, someone might ask you, "How on earth did you accomplish *that?*" You might not know yourself. Not surprisingly, you may respond, "I don't know. It just happened." *That*'s courage.

experiment

Study a role model. I have adopted Eleanor Roosevelt's words, "You must do the thing you think you cannot do," as my mantra. Give yourself the gift of one or many role models and adopt their coping strategies as your own. Whether it's Helen Keller or Helen Gurley Brown, your role models can engender the kind of risk-taking, courage-grabbing inspiration you need.

Look in your own backyard. Some of your closest friends and acquaintances may be the most courageous people around, though you may not even know it. Begin to pay attention to the challenges other people face on a daily or weekly basis. Maybe a friend has endured months of chemotherapy but still needs to keep her household running. Or the neighbor who cares for an aging parent, or the woman you know who's raising children on her own either out of choice or because her partner suddenly died. If we stop just for a moment to think about how others handle adversity, we can usually see the world with a little more clarity, compassion, and yes, courage, too.

Take itsy-bitsy baby steps. Just because you're an adult doesn't mean you can't move slowly. Instead of setting yourself up for failure by doing too much at once, think of the strides you'll make by sampling a little courage one small bite at a time. If a room full of strangers—some of whom might support your dreams—makes you wobbly-kneed, look for two friendly faces, people who seem receptive to meeting a newcomer, and warmly introduce yourself. Be ready to ask questions, exchange business cards, and provide a little data about yourself as well. After you leave, focus on what you did right, not what you may have forgotten to say. Later, expand your review and think about what you might do the next time around.

Zigzag down the mountain. The fastest route isn't always necessary. My daughter recently told me about a time when she rode the ski lift and mistakenly disembarked on the farthest and topmost hill. "I meant to get off sooner," she said, "but I still wanted to go down the hill." "How did you have the courage?" I asked, both of us knowing that if this had happened to me, I would've removed my boots and walked down. "I zigzagged because I really wanted to do it," she said. Sometimes we have to take the long way. Maybe there's a detour—missed opportunity, unexpected interruption— and we have to find another way to return home. Or perhaps we make a deal with ourselves: "I'll go down this mountain, but only if I can do it my way." We may zigzag for a while until one day, after we've slipped down the mountain ten times in a row, we realize that not only are we capable of taking on more, we actually crave the challenge.

practice

It takes courage for me to:

1. _____

_____

2. _____

_____

3. _____

_____

In the past, I've been afraid to:

1. _____

_____

2. _____

_____

3. _____

_____

When I listen, I can hear my inner voice encourage me to:

1. _____

_____

2. _____

_____

3. _____

_____

affirm

Like love, my courage is infinite and alive.

When I'm (a little) courageous, I

_____

_____

~ week 10 ~

Talk About It

Don't tell anyone what you wished for.
—*Traditional poor advice*

ask

1. Do I keep my wishes and dreams to myself?
2. What stops me from sharing my dreams?
3. Am I afraid of what others might say?
4. Am I afraid of receiving criticism?
5. Who *could* I talk to about my wishes and dreams?
6. Do I equate talking about my passions with being self-absorbed?
7. Do I really believe that by talking about my wishes and dreams, they won't come true?

How many times have you heard someone say, "Don't tell anyone what you wish for because then it won't come true!"? Well, as of today—at this very moment—you are no longer bound by such silly and superstitious advice. From now on, I want you to look for ways to talk about your wishes and dreams, to coax them into the light, and to gently extract them from their secret spaces hidden deep inside.

When we keep our dreams locked away, we are feeding that insatiable monster called "fear." If you tether down your dreams, they will never soar. When you deny your dreams a voice, you quell any hope for turning what you want into what is yours.

Once you decide that your wishes and dreams should come out to play, you're likely to make some discoveries. Some will be stunning, others puzzling, but all will intrigue. You will probably find, for instance, that people actually will listen and may even ask questions to find out more. Indeed, people may not laugh or say, "That's impossible!" You may hear four of the sweetest words imaginable: "What a good idea."

If you've been reluctant to give your dreams an audience, ask yourself why. Were you worried that you might not adequately articulate your dreams? Did you think that others would equate your dreams with arrogance? Become an objective observer whose feelings and preconceived notions are out of bounds. Draw a face for each of your fears, too—fear of success, fear of embarrassment, fear of failure. Assign a voice to each fear. Ask yourself, "Who's talking?" Perhaps you're hearing an old teacher, a vexing voice from high school chemistry. Or maybe the words belong to a former love, someone who was unable to live with your ever-widening wings. It could be a boss, a sibling, or a parent. Give yourself permission to prove them wrong.

As you introduce your wishes and dreams to the world, remember to be open to the comments and questions that are likely to follow. Some people will be genuinely interested in your passions; your enthusiasm could touch others in ways that you might not have imagined. For instance, when people ask how you got your idea, by all means tell them. Don't be afraid of someone stealing your idea unless of course you're under a contractual obligation of some sort. On the other hand, if your intuition instructs you to share just a portion of the whole picture, honor that inner voice and keep what you need to yourself.

Sharing with others is cathartic and can restore your sense of well-being and belonging. You might be standing in a room full of strangers and after one person speaks openly and earnestly about a particularly profound experience, you feel at once relieved and part of something bigger than yourself, something meaningful and expansive. When Dorothy Foltz-Gray began running races again, she was apprehensive and doubted her abilities. "I hadn't run a race in a while and I was a little intimidated when I arrived to find all these runners who seemed to be in better shape. To me, they all looked like storks with six-foot-long legs," she says. "A little while later, I was sitting on the bleachers and another woman turned to me and said, 'I'm really nervous. I haven't run in a long time.' This stranger's words and her compassion immediately made me feel better, and I realized that everyone was probably feeling some degree of flutter. Even my fear became universal, something that ultimately wouldn't hold me back after all." Similarly, maybe a friend shares an embarrassing story and, as you listen to her laugh heartily at her recollection, you realize you're not alone on the imperfect path that is *your* life.

experiment

Tell them something they don't know. Pat Giovacchini is the author of *Christmas Cook-Ease*, a cookbook with recipes for more than a hundred kinds of cookies. At a meeting at her local chamber of commerce she shared the origin of her longstanding love for baking. "I was seventeen at the time, trying to think of a Christmas present I could bring to my boyfriend's mother, who I was meeting for the first time," she said. "I didn't have a big budget, so I made cookies and I've been doing it ever since." Her words remind us that the serendipitous coupling of our circumstances with our dreams could significantly change the course of our lives. So, the next time you're at a gathering, ask people, "Tell us something we don't know," and be sure to let everyone in on your wishes and dreams, too.

Tell yourself about your dreams. One day—probably best when you're alone—start speaking about your dreams. Be your best, most attentive audience. If you feel awkward, just laugh out loud at your silliness, then compose yourself and get serious. How does it feel to hear your voice giving breath to your wishes and dreams? Are you afraid? Are you surprised? Are you more committed than ever?

Build a platform. You don't need a Ph.D. or a byline on a book to speak on your specialty. If you're interested in turning a hobby into a career, or would simply like to grow your business, consider creating a presentation that would appeal to prospective customers. Marcia Sacks is a professional writer and astrologer. In addition to her private consultations Marcia spends time teaching astrology, meditation, and inner work for self-healing. "My students are my best clients, because they understand what astrology is all about." Contact your local park district, school district, library, church, synagogue, and other outlets for adult learning to inquire about teaching opportunities.

Learn and practice the art of conversation. When you talk about your dreams and wishes you are inviting commentary not only about your life but about your listeners' lives as well. I'm sure you're familiar with the old adage that it is far better to listen than to talk. If that's true, however, how can you possibly "talk about it"? You don't have to talk about your dreams without a break.

Indeed, you will lose your listeners' interest if you overwhelm them with your stories without giving them a chance to respond. If you catch yourself talking too much, pause and say something like, "You've been listening so well to me. I'd like to hear more about what you're doing now." Just be aware of this and you'll do fine.

Express it your way. Verbal expression is just one of the ways you can talk about your wishes and dreams. Collages, photographs, and original drawings can also be your media for expression. Photographer Nancy Watts is well known for her portraits, yet it's her original stationery that I find truly stunning. Not too long ago, I bought five spectacular cards, all featuring Nancy's original images from nature. I've been able to part with only one, though eventually I will send the remaining four as well—one way of sharing Nancy's work with others who might not otherwise know about her. The cards may not be her cash cow, but creating and making them available to others gives Nancy an outlet for expressing another side of her creativity.

practice

I'd be comfortable sharing these little-known facts about myself:

1. _____

_____

2. _____

_____

3. _____

_____

Here are three things I remember about a recent conversation during which I talked about my wishes and dreams:

1. _____

_____

2. _____

_____

3. _____

_____

I can hone my conversational skills by:

1. _____

_____

2. _____

_____

3. _____

_____

affirm

The more I can talk about the things that matter to me most, the more I trust the process of my life.

When I talk about it, I

_____

_____

~ week 11 ~

Harness the Power of Prayer

> The life of prayer is so great and various there is something in it for everyone. It is like a garden which grows everything, from alpines to potatoes.
>
> —Evelyn Underhill, *Collected Papers of Evelyn Underhill* (1946), edited by Lucy Menzies

ask

1. Can I pray without expecting a specific outcome?
2. As a child, what did prayer mean to me?
3. How do I feel when I pray with others?
4. Do I ever doubt the power of prayer?
5. Do I believe the power of prayer is infinite?
6. In the past, why have I prayed?
7. How can prayer help me wish, dream, and do?

You don't have to be a religious person to harness the power of prayer. If you're heart is in it, then it's prayer. You can pray anywhere. Praying in the shower is as sacred as doing so in a church or synagogue. Sometimes, though, we need the harmony that's created when we pray with others.

When we harness the power of prayer, we wrap our wishes and dreams with possibilities. Instead of limiting ourselves and cutting off our access to what we can't necessarily anticipate, we maintain open minds and hearts. But that's not always so easy, especially if the results you were hoping for are not forthcoming. Prayer is not about asking for certain results. Prayer helps us embrace the outcome whether it's good or bad. We pray for strength, understanding, patience, and whatever else we need to pursue our dreams. Prayer clears away the debris that often prevents us from recognizing opportunities. Sometimes when I pray for clarity I find myself standing nose-to-nose with something so raw and truthful that it takes my breath away. I may not always know what I'm praying for, yet somehow this private conversation with God seems to underscore my enduring faith in the world.

We can pray anywhere at any time, yet we can never schedule an answer to our prayers. When I was in labor with my son, the pain was manageable at first. I knew the birth would be nothing like what I'd experienced with my daughter, who'd been born by emergency cesarean section. As the contractions became more intense, I began to pray. I prayed for the pain to subside. It got worse. I prayed that I was at Disney World, but I remained in the same room. I prayed that the nurse would give me drugs. She didn't. Later, when my doctor breezed in to ask how I was doing, I said, "Just shoot me." And then my son—as he will tell anyone, including any number of people standing behind us in a line—came shooting out "like a football." Miraculously, the pain stopped. I was at Disney World after all. I am convinced that prayer, timing, and the laws of nature all converged to bring forth that new life. My prayers were answered but not nearly in the way that I had imagined.

As you consider the ways you might harness the power of prayer, remember always that you must do it your way. It's not complicated. Indeed, it's as simple and natural as yearning. Think of prayer as a means of opening up and expanding your possibilities.

experiment

Define your moment of spiritual well-being. You can harness the power of prayer by recalling specific moments of spiritual well-being. Such a moment occurred when I was seventeen. I'd spent the summer in Kenya and had climbed a small mountain with a friend. I stared for the longest time at the scene before me: lush green stillness except for the smoke that rose from the mud huts far below. I still get goose bumps each time I recall that afternoon. Once you define your moment, keep it in mind. The memory might have nothing to do with where you are right now, but it could help redirect a powerless feeling into one with more strength and resolve.

Pick one ritual. Commit to one spiritual ritual a week. Light candles, read a prayer, attend a religious service, or perform a good deed. Anything that invokes hope and possibility will keep you tethered to your journey and further your progress.

Keep prayer nearby. Many years ago, after a family member was diagnosed with a terminal illness, I met with a rabbi who gave me a copy of a "prayer for the body." I relied on this prayer to help me channel my sorrow. For that reason, I folded up the prayer and placed it inside my wallet, where it has stayed for years. I know it is nearby and that alone helps me harness its power. Find a prayer that speaks to you and keep it close.

Write your own prayers. In addition to using prayers from books and other sources, you can write your own. Pick up a small spiral notebook at the store or a journal reserved for your lines of verse.

practice

In the past, I've relied on prayer to:

I. _____

_____

2. _____

_____

3. _____

_____

Prayer helps me focus less on outcomes and more on the moment by:

I. _____

_____

2. _____

_____

3. _____

_____

Today, I'm going to pray for:

I. _____

_____

2. _____

_____

3. _____

_____

affirm

Prayer accompanies me on all my journeys and reminds me that the most sacred part of me will always remain intact.

When I harness the power of prayer, I

_____

_____

~ week 12 ~

Learn to Let Go

Security is when everything is settled, when nothing can happen to you; security is the denial of life.
—Germaine Greer, *The Female Eunuch* (1971)

ask

1. As a child, what did I learn about control?
2. What situations do I try to control?
3. Do I generally associate letting go with giving up?
4. How do I feel when I try to maintain control?
5. How do I feel when I do let go?
6. Do I have positive or negative associations with the word *surrender*?
7. Am I willing to learn to let go?

How often do you find yourself becoming more anxious by the second because something is out of your control? It happens to me, but as time goes on I realize that in most cases it's best to learn to let it go. Whether I'm trying to control my children, my husband, or a situation, the fact is that what I want ultimately has little to do with the outcome. Ironically, when we stop trying to control everything we're actually in a better position to *take* control of our lives. Several years ago Laurel Yourke's mother was in a coma that lasted nearly two weeks. The doctors said she had a 1 to 2 percent chance of survival. "We were very close then and I was crazed with grief, anxiety, and helplessness," says Laurel, a faculty associate in the University of Wisconsin, Madison, Department of Liberal Studies and the Arts. "I flew from Madison to New York to be with her and was prepared to stay, but my partner persuaded me to bring work home and return to Wisconsin for a few days. I was ambivalent but decided it was the right thing to do. One day we drove to Sauk City, a place known for its eagles. So for about two hours we stood in the cold and simply watched these magnificent birds dive and soar above the lapis-blue river, glittering in the sun. I was convinced that I wouldn't be able to relax, calm down, or stop crying, yet after a half hour of winging along with those eagles I was prepared to accept whatever lay ahead. I let go." Happily, Laurel's mother came out of the coma. To this day, Laurel is convinced that on some level her mother's survival was tied to her experience at the river. "I still believe that without my loving partner's insistence that we take that drive, this story might have ended differently." Remember that giving in is not the same as giving up, and letting go doesn't mean that you can't still believe.

Learning how to let go may feel incredibly uncomfortable. The notion that we're more together if we have more control—over our spending, eating, and doing—is still so ingrained in us. Yet, it is this need for control that ultimately paralyzes us and prevents us from turning the lives we're living into the lives we want.

For Pat DeLuca, a training consultant, it's taken many years and several painful lessons to learn that control, for her, is an illusion. As a single parent, juggling a consulting business and the joys and demands of home, Pat couldn't do everything. "First, I needed to know what I hated doing, either because I wasn't good at it or because I just didn't want to do it. So I finally hired a bookkeeper. I hated keeping track of my checkbook and I'm not very good at it either. I made big mistakes and tore my hair out trying to fix them. My accountant finally advised me to find someone I could trust, who would meet my standards and take on the task. It's taken me many years and several bookkeepers, but today I have someone who's really sharp, detail oriented, and knows all those numbers. Now I pay her to maintain both my business books and my home checking account. And life is a lot easier—I don't worry about what I've forgotten to enter, the bills are finally getting paid on time, and, unless I do something really stupid, I don't bounce checks!" Pat's bookkeeper comes in every two weeks and in the big picture has saved Pat both time and money. "I gain a lot more time to do the things that are important to me and I pay a lot less in late fees," she adds. As you examine your tendencies to maintain control, ask yourself, among other things, whether your fear of giving in helps or hinders your ability to wish, dream, and do.

experiment

Choose your company wisely. Sometimes it is the people around us who dictate our behavior. If we surround ourselves with people who need to have control, we might think that's standard. If your circle sweeps you up into a whirlwind of control and power, try to step out onto the other side. Observe the scene before you and ask yourself if that's really the way you want to live. Don't expect to change your behavior without some slow and steady work. Identifying a harmful characteristic that before seemed innocuous can be startling. Be compassionate with yourself as you move further away.

Focus on the means, not the end. As a writer, I fantasize every now and then about bestsellerdom. But you know what? Too much of that prevents me from what really matters—writing. It also keeps me far from the moment. Since I don't want to miss the moment, I try to embrace the process whenever I can. Sometimes I have to consciously breathe or I'll need a good grounding from a friend with some perspective. If you find that you just can't let go, loosen your grip on your past and your future and tie yourself exclusively to where you are at that particular moment. A new perspective is likely to make a landing right before your very eyes.

Give away the training wheels. Some of us moved directly from a tricycle to a two-wheeler. Others, like me, relied on a set of training wheels to stretch out the transition. Yet, even after graduating to a big-kid bike those training wheels sat up on a shelf. Why did I hold on to those wheels? We hold on to sources of support that we really don't need. If you've been holding on to something that helped you in the past but is clearly unnecessary now, give it away. Maybe it's an old piece of office equipment or even an outdated power suit that got you through your first few jobs. Keeping support systems around like mementos can prevent you from progressing to the next important step.

Repeat after me: "It's not my table." This is my all-time favorite expression spoken by my husband when he separates himself from someone else's stuff. For me, it evokes an image of a dinner table laden with dishes and the remainder of food after a formidable feast. Just as we might push our plates a few inches toward the center and shift our chairs in another direction, we must occasionally do the same with people. An old argument, points of view that will never meet, anger that cannot be resolved—in these situations, sometimes the best response is to walk away and let it go. You may be giving up control, but you'll gain unparalleled peace of mind.

Delegate. Jettisoning some responsibilities is one way to let go. Yet, it usually takes a close friend or two or a supervisor to persuade us to delegate some of those duties. If we're under great pressure we might cave in and slowly hand off certain duties to colleagues, children, and partners. Ideally, though, we should learn how to delegate *before* our lives spin out of control. Hand off a parent/teacher appointment to your partner when work demands your full attention. Show your children how to put away their laundry. If you head a committee, assign others specific jobs that have a beginning and an end. If you honestly believe that you're indispensable, you will struggle in your efforts to delegate. So try examining your feelings about how much you do for others and whether or not your relationships might benefit by your stepping back a little so that others can do for themselves. You'll be doing everyone a favor.

practice

In the past, it's been difficult to let go because:

1. _____

   _____

2. _____

   _____

3. _____

   _____

I would like to let go of the following:

1. _____
   _____

2. _____
   _____

3. _____
   _____

Letting go will enable me to:

1. _____
   _____

2. _____
   _____

3. _____
   _____

affirm

I'm able to focus on my dreams because I've stopped worrying about taking care of others when they need to take care of themselves.

When I learn to let go, I

_____

_____

~ week 13 ~

Ask for Help

I always wanted to be somebody. . . . If I've made it, it's half because I was game to take a wicked amount of punishment along the way and half because there were an awful lot of people who cared enough to help me.
—Althea Gibson, *I Always Wanted to Be Somebody* (1958)

ask

1. Is it hard for me to admit that I need help?
2. Is self-sufficiency a high priority for me?
3. Was I taught to ask for help in emergencies only?
4. How do I feel when people ask me for help?
5. Do I know how to ask for help so that people understand what I need?
6. How good am I at recruiting support from my family?
7. Can't I just wish, dream, and do on my own?

When asked, many of us are happy to offer our help. It feels good to be needed, but it's particularly fulfilling when our efforts actually advance someone else's endeavors. Yet, when it is our turn to ask for help, many of us give up our place in line. Instead of taking our turn, fair and square, we walk away or go to the end of the queue.

Why do we give up this way? In some cases, we become comfortable with the line. Waiting becomes a safe and secure buffer zone. Some people believe that asking for help is a sign of weakness. Even our originality is called into question when we canvas people for their opinions, as if seeking other points of view will diminish our own ideas. In some cases, we may just be afraid of rejection. What if someone says, "No, I'm sorry. I can't help you"? Then what? Well, you move on. It's that simple.

Maybe we just don't like to burden other people. Certainly, if you ask the same people for help too often they may feel put upon and even a little resentful. Some of us don't like to be indebted to others for *anything*. We avoid asking so that we won't feel beholden. But for the most part, seeking support will help you to more easily turn the life you're living into the life you want. Delegating household duties, asking for assistance on the job, and recruiting your friends and family for emotional sustenance are essential if you want to reenvision and change your life.

Jeffrey Hedquist, who heads a radio productions and audio marketing company in Fairfield, Iowa, introduced a simple, but significant, office upgrade by networking the e-mail. "Before the upgrade I was the e-mail point of contact," he says. "Now, our audio engineer can send and receive MP3s and any recording-related correspondence. Our office manager can send out sales letters, help manage our e-mail list, and follow up collection calls, also through e-mail. Our casting director and director of client services can receive and send scripts, proposals, and press releases. Plus, everyone can use the Web for research."

Prior to the upgrade Jeffrey performed these tasks, leaving him little time for strategic planning, web site development, and other marketing activities. "I'm even getting more sleep," he adds.

Clearly, asking for help is not easy. At first, it feels terribly uncomfortable, like you've got your pants on backward. You can still walk okay, but you feel ridiculous. When we ask for help, we feel vulnerable. Yet, that vulnerability is really a form of truth, not a sign of weakness. Some of our best leaders in business and government are successful because they've surrounded themselves with a strong and steady support system. Icons like Lee Iacocca, Mary Kay, and Bill Gates built success teams that allowed them to bring their visions to life. You can do the same with similar results. Seeking emotional support from others is not a display of incompetence; it's a demonstration of your intelligence, whether you're trying to add to your base of knowledge or learn something new. When we ask for help we're acknowledging the splendor and fundamental need for a circle of giving. Besides, some people love to share their experiences, which in many cases will be all you need. It's rewarding for you *and* for them. Eventually, you will learn how to ask for help with grace and diplomacy. It will feel as right as your favorite pair of shoes.

experiment

Be direct. Many years ago a friendship suffered because I neglected to be direct and honest when I asked for help. Instead of speaking in precise terms, I asked for help in a roundabout way that left my intentions and needs unclear. When I didn't receive the help, I was hurt and my friend was puzzled. When you ask for help be clear so that people know exactly what you want. If they can help, they usually will. If they can't, they'll let you know that, too. But don't use hazy language just because you're afraid or uncomfortable. This will lead only to misunderstandings, which in the long run will be a waste of time for everyone.

Be gracious no matter what. When you ask for help, try to be gracious no matter what. "Thanks anyway" (with a smile) works wonders even when someone says "no." Pouting only makes matters worse. Remember that most people want to help but in some cases can't because of all sorts of circumstances beyond their control. Don't make people feel worse by dwelling on their inability (or unwillingness) to provide support. Besides, just because people can't help doesn't mean they don't want to help. Indeed, if you respond graciously, they may be more inclined to think of someone else who can help. They may even reconsider and offer to help you after all. Your patience and understanding (versus impatience and resentment) will almost always be in your best interest.

Reciprocate when you can. When I was pregnant with my son I had to go on bed rest after a shaky and uncertain week in the hospital. Friends cooked, drove, and took over other duties that under normal circumstances would've been difficult to jettison off to others. Overwhelmed by their generosity, I constantly sought ways to reciprocate. Of course, that was nearly impossible since I wasn't supposed to be moving around. My doctor finally said one day, "Leslie, no one is helping so that you can help them back. They're helping because they want to." Maybe it was his white jacket or his kind but exasperated tone that got my attention. From that moment on I decided that I'd reciprocate after I'd given birth. To this day, I am grateful for my friends' generosity in deeds but even more thankful for their roles in helping to bring a healthy baby into the world.

Recruit family support with compassion and understanding. Often, it's the people closest to us who have the hardest time providing support. Kids and spouses may feel threatened by your goals and wonder where they fit in. They may worry, for instance, that your dreams will take up too much time. Spouses, especially, may fear how your dreams will affect the family income. Partners, but especially children, may be unable to articulate their worries about what will become of them when you successfully turn the life you're living into the life you want. Listen to their concerns and assure them that you will continue to be an important part of their lives. Let them know how meaningful their help is and show your gratitude on a regular basis. This is a good time, too, to ask how *you* can help *them* to wish, dream, and do.

practice

In the past, asking for help was difficult because it made me feel:

1. _____

_____

2. _____

_____

3. _____

_____

I'm learning how to ask for help so that I can:

1. _____

_____

2. _____

_____

3. _____

_____

This week I'm going to ask for help in the following ways:

1. _____

_____

2. _____

_____

3. _____

_____

affirm

Instead of welling up with resentment for not getting what I want, I conspire with the world to help me turn the life I'm living into the life I want.

When I ask for help, I

_____

_____

Make Peace with Your Past

One faces the future with one's past.
—Pearl S. Buck, *What America Means to Me*
(1943)

ask

1. Does my past limit my thinking about the future?
2. Does my past prevent me from gaining new insights?
3. Does my history prevent me from changing and growing?
4. Do I give old, negative voices too much play?
5. Can I outgrow my past and release its power over me?
6. Can I distinguish between negative beliefs and negative realities?
7. Can I turn what I want into what is mine without making peace with my past?

Most of us have something in our past with which we struggle: relationships, criticism, tragedies, missed opportunities, almost unforgivable mistakes. When these struggles prevent us from creating a fulfilling future, we become prisoners of our pasts. You can't fix every unresolved issue, you can't right every wrong, and it's wasteful to regret what never happened. But you can make peace with your past—if you're willing and ready to take a good look at where you're from. Only then can you derive some perspective and clarity. Imagine yourself on the outside looking in—observe what was happening as if you're watching an old movie. Once you revisit the painful parts and perform the necessary healing work, it becomes easier to walk away and tell yourself, "That's a place where I used to live."

People who've turned the lives they're living into the lives they want often experience "aha" moments that beautifully put their pasts into crystal-clear perspective. That it takes years to realize is almost beside the point. You might be reading something that suddenly reminds you of something that happened when you were thirteen or thirty-three, or perhaps the person you're talking with says something that takes you back into a memory and all at once it hits you: "Oh, here's what was going on then," or, "This is what she meant when she said such-and-such." Jay Mulvaney's "aha" moment came at a crucial point and quickly turned the worst situation he'd ever experienced into a life filled with health, harmony, and happiness. "I once lost my job as a direct result of an addiction that I had steadfastly refused to acknowledge," he says. "'It's not hurting anyone,' I thought. What I couldn't see at the time was that it was hurting me, enormously. A quarter million dollars a year salary, with all its attendant perks, gone; the prestige I found self-acceptance in, evaporated; the security of a place to go every day and a routine to follow, vanished.

"Lying alone in the bed that night, I saw not destruction, but opportunity—to start my life anew, to fix the behavior and patterns of self-destruction that had shackled me for forty-five years. I literally heard a voice inside me say 'fix it,'" says Jay, author of *Diana & Jackie: Maidens, Mothers, Myths.*

With the help of loving family and friends, Jay took control of

his life and embarked on a journey that has led to creative fulfill-
ment, professional recognition, and a life full of honest feelings.
"Today when I'm happy, I'm honestly happy—and when I'm sad,
I'm honestly sad," he says.

Recognizing self-defeating behaviors often occurs after a careful analysis of what happened years ago. I believe with all my heart
that a gentle excavation of our pasts can ultimately shake us free
from certain demons and then, finally, set into motion a series of
promising life events. Think of your past as a long, well-worn
strand of yarn that's unraveled from an old, handmade sweater.
The sweater is probably gone forever, but you can make something
new—something warm—with the wool that remains.

experiment

Find your past in your present. Sometimes the easiest way to recognize your assets and liabilities is to think about where you've
come from. Make a list of your strongest personality traits. For
each trait, note from whom you most likely inherited or learned
that characteristic. You're likely to discover some things about your
present life that are steeped in history. For instance, you might
have learned how to speak up by observing your mother do the
same for herself. Also, consider the influence of parents, siblings,
friends, teachers, and colleagues.

Think of one thing you'd like to change. Bringing on change is a
subtle way of making peace with your past. You can say you've
always been a certain way, but until you make up your mind to
make the necessary shift, you and your past will always be in conflict. Would you like to finally get organized? Do you want to lose

a little weight? Do you wish you would listen more when people talk? Choose one and work on it. Slowly, add more to your list.

Forgive if you can. When you make peace with your past, you practice forgiveness for hurting others and for hurting yourself. If you're having trouble releasing others' hurtful deeds, look inward to see if you've forgiven yourself. Usually, this is a much harder task but one that will teach you to soften and become more compassionate.

Make a paper chain. Remember how paper chains could instantly turn the plain and drab into something festive and whimsical? Well, you can do the same for your past. Gather some paper (colored sheets of construction paper are nice but not necessary), scissors, and some glue or tape. Cut out several strips of paper and write on each piece an event or circumstance that might be preventing you from moving forward. Once you've made the chain and reminded yourself of those pesky memories, rip it to shreds or ceremoniously burn it. In other words, break the chain.

practice

When old hurts arise, I feel:

1. _____
   _____

2. _____
   _____

3. _____
   _____

When a friend criticizes me, it brings back memories of:

1. _____

_____

2. _____

_____

3. _____

_____

If I could fill up a blank page from my past, it would say:

1. _____

_____

2. _____

_____

3. _____

_____

affirm

Instead of playing the victim, I become a student and observer of my past.

When I make peace with my past, I

_____

_____

~ week 15 ~

Cherish and Honor
Your Work Space

In my studio I'm as happy as a cow in her stall.
—Louise Nevelson, *Dawns + Dusks* (1976)

ask

1. Do I feel at home in my work space?
2. Do I feel isolated in my work space?
3. What would make my space a pleasant place to be?
4. Have I surrounded myself with objects that have meaning for me?
5. Do I keep my space organized?
6. Am I more productive in a calm environment or in one with more activity?
7. Does the atmosphere support my needs?

Instead of seeking perfection in your work space, try first and foremost to create an area that helps you focus. If bare walls keep you tethered to your purpose, then by all means go for the minimalist look. If, on the other hand, the paintbrush of a three-year-old inspires you, surround yourself with whimsy and color. In either case—and in between—make sure that your space reflects who you really are and gives you a sense of self. On my desk, among other things, are a handmade ebony carving I picked up as an exchange student in Kenya and a can of Pick-up Sticks that reminds me of the importance of play. On the wall before me is a picture of my family at Disney World, a love note (and apology) from my husband, and numerous pictures created by my children. I feel cradled there and am able to concentrate, in part, because I am surrounded by representations of warmth and love.

Whether you're sitting in a windowless office or tucked into a corner of your dining room, creating a meaningful work space is essential for infusing quality into your wishes and dreams. You may not always have the resources—financial or otherwise—to create the perfect work space. But with some imagination, planning, and a little compromise, you can make a space that embraces harmony and balance and promotes a sense of well-being under the best (no deadlines) and worst (many deadlines) circumstances. Naturally, you will know from a visual perspective what turns you on (and off) about your present work space. But don't overlook the way you feel when you enter your space. A visceral reaction—a tightening in your stomach, for instance—can reveal a lot about how well matched you are with your environment.

Even if you go to an office you might need to bring work home at night, or perhaps you want to devote your evening hours to finding the work of your dreams so that you can quit your Monday-through-Friday gig. If you don't have a home office you can still get work done. A kitchen table is still a wonderful surface for spreading things out. Your bed can be the perfect writing nest. And shelves and boxes make great storage. When the weather is warm I occasionally take my work into the backyard.

experiment

Give your space power. Consider the power of feng shui, the traditional Chinese art of cultivating spiritual power in your dwelling. Learn about this ancient wisdom so that you can incorporate its concept of harmony and space in your work environment (see Suggested Reading). For example, water and glass are associated with career and finding your life path, so put a glass vase of fresh flowers in your work space to lead you in the right direction.

Make it mobile. When my home is overrun with people and I absolutely, positively must get work done, I have the option of camping in a nearby coffeehouse or setting up in my friend Judith's lovely home. Think about where you might create a temporary work space. A bench in a nearby park, a room in a museum, a favorite café, and even your local library offer opportunities to work in fresh surroundings.

Buy quality when you can. You deserve to work amid quality surroundings. The more time you spend in a work space, the more important it becomes for you to enjoy your environment. When we moved from upstate New York to the Midwest I had to leave behind a beautiful and functional handmade, built-in desk. Instead of "making do" with a flimsy substitute I splurged on a solid wood desk. It was an instinctive buy, too, because I knew that each time I walked into my work space I'd be drawn to the warmth and sturdiness of my desk. In the long run, those less-expensive purchases—the "deals"—actually become costly mistakes for your soul and your wallet.

Create order. Books, workshops, and special products designed to facilitate orderly home and work environments are available everywhere. You can even hire an expert organizer to assess your surroundings and offer solutions for clearing up and paring down. Do it in steps so you're not overwhelmed.

Clip and save. Take some time to sift through magazines that offer ideas for serene living. Create a scrapbook of the photographs that catch your eye and provide inspiration. Borrow an idea or re-create a whole room.

practice

My work space isn't always adequate because:

1. _____

   _____

2. _____

   _____

3. _____

   _____

The following possessions give meaning to my work space:

1. _____

   _____

2. _____

   _____

3. _____

_____

In the future, my work space will be more:

1. _____

_____

2. _____

_____

3. _____

_____

affirm

When I honor and cherish my work space, I do the same for my dreams.

When I honor and cherish my work space,

_____

_____

~ week 16 ~

Break the Rules

Experience shows that exceptions are as true as rules.
—Edith Ronald Mirrieless, *Story Writing* (1947)

ask

1. Am I afraid to break the rules? What am I afraid of?
2. Do I equate breaking the rules with being too self-indulgent?
3. Would my disregard for certain rules upset other people? How?
4. Do I generally agree with conventional wisdom or am I constantly questioning the status quo?
5. How often do I break the rules?
6. Would bending a rule here and there make my life any easier?
7. What are the rules that prevent me from turning the life I'm living into the life I want?

Some people are always breaking the rules. It's in their blood. Others can't function without them; to suggest that a rule be broken is practically blasphemous. It's a dicey business to tamper with convention, but if you want to wish, dream, and do, consider becoming comfortable with bending, redefining, and otherwise breaking a few rules.

How do we become rule breakers? In some cases, it's sort of a seat-of-the-pants experience. Perhaps you weren't planning on making an exception but you just couldn't help yourself. Or maybe you knew from the start that you and a particularly menacing rule were never going to see eye-to-eye. You might even have been told to *wing it*: "Do it your way—just get it done." Ultimately, I believe that is why we break the rules. We need to get things done and the only way to make that happen is, from time to time, to turn our backs on the rules. From the time she was in high school—perhaps even earlier—Robin Blakely, creative director and president of Livingston Communications, has stood face-to-face with certain rules. "The only rule I commonly break is what I call the 'you can't because we don't' rule," she says. "In college I wanted to intern at a local radio station, but they said I couldn't because they didn't have the program. So I created the one I wanted and became the intern. Later, as a parent of two asthmatic kids, I wanted my school district to adopt a special program for children with chronic asthma. They said they couldn't, which was almost like a dare. I created a plan and put it into action. I knew that this particular rule was made for me to break. Subsequently, breaking that particularly menacing rule changed my life. Today, I have healthy children, an amazing husband, and a company with extraordinary clients and exciting projects from around the country.

"I honestly believe that real rules are intended to protect and support people, never handicap them or oppress them."

Naturally, you don't want to step outside the law or intentionally harm or hurt another human being. I do recommend, however, that, like Robin, you reassess your adherence to certain prescripts that for one reason or another have less and less relevance to your life. Breaking the rules is about asserting your independence and becoming the person you are meant to be.

You may not know it, but each time you break with tradition in order to live your life with more truth and validity, you become a bit of a revolutionary. Most people confine themselves to doing things the way they've always been done. But it's the risk takers, mistake makers, and rule breakers who wish, dream, and do with verve and conviction. Sometimes the people we admire most seem sheepish when they're asked how they can do what they do so well. Teachers, for example, who perform miracles every day, often respond this way when parents marvel over their skills and talents. Celebrities who comment on their struggles to the top often tell us how they challenged the naysayers and others who doubted their abilities. "I do the opposite of what I'm told." "I broke a few rules along the way." "If you tell me I can't, I can almost guarantee that I will." In other words, they wouldn't have it any other way.

experiment

Speak the truth. Too often we're advised to speak the truth but when we do so the reception isn't as warm as we might have hoped. You can speak honestly, however, without necessarily hurting those around you. For example, first tell someone what you liked before you criticize. Say something like, "I like the strategy you're suggesting, but I'm not sure how we can apply it to this particular scenario." Or, instead of attacking someone, first accept partial responsibility. You could say, "I have a lot going on in my life right now, so I might not be as receptive as you'd like. . . ." To wish, dream, and do with success, you must be willing to shed certain secrets so that you can more easily—and with less fear—speak the truth. Withholding the truth may not be as blatant as lying, but it is disingenuous just the same. Speak the truth about your wishes and dreams, and your flaws as well, and you're likely to discover that we're all pretty much the same and can help one another grow.

Don't do as you're told. Sometimes when we share our passions we get advice from all corners. One person may instruct you to max out your credit card to finance your dream. Another may advise you to take care of other business before you pursue something so extraordinary and challenging. Don't always do as you're told even if the advice seems sound. It might have worked for someone else, but your needs are distinct and may require a different solution.

Do less even though there's more. These days many of us are expected to do more with fewer and fewer resources. "Do more with less" is the not-so-new clarion call in many industries. Sometimes, though, it's possible—and preferable—to do less even though there's more. We will always be surrounded by more than we can absorb. Information and all the things that money can buy hit us from every direction, but that doesn't mean we need to hold on to everything that comes our way. Breaking the rules will help you focus more sharply on creating the life you want.

practice

When I follow all the rules, I sometimes miss out on:

1. _____

_____

2. _____

_____

3. _____

_____

I could move closer to my dreams if I could break or bend the following three rules:

1. _____

_____

2. _____

_____

3. _____

_____

Breaking the rules will help me become more:

1. _____

_____

2. _____

_____

3. _____

_____

affirm

When I break the rules, I infuse my life with flexibility and a new perspective.

When I break the rules, I

_____

_____

~ week 17 ~

Study Your Lines

*Language exerts hidden power, like the moon
on the tides.*

—Rita Mae Brown,
Starting from Scratch (1988)

ask

1. Do I say what's on my mind or do I say what I think people want to hear?
2. Do I occasionally say more than I should?
3. Do I sometimes agree to do something because I can't think of a way to say "no"?
4. Do I ever give unsolicited advice?
5. Am I more likely to say what I don't mean when I feel under pressure?
6. How can I combine a rehearsed response with language that seems spontaneous?
7. Who do I know whose self-determination is exhibited in the way she studies and speaks her lines?

Wouldn't life be simpler if for every difficult situation we could reach into our pockets for a script that would guide us to say the right thing? If only we could consult our own writer who could accompany us into every uncertain predicament and whisper into our ears the perfect lines. We'd be self-possessed, calm, and pre-pared for a host of unsettling circumstances.

A lot of the mistakes we make—the moments when we're not exactly at our best—often occur because we're just not prepared. We don't know what to say. We can't believe what someone else has said. We're dumbstruck or we say dumb things back. Afterward, we review the scene, sometimes over and over again until it dissipates and becomes a memory, at which point we begin to insert the lines we wish we'd used.

No matter how hard I work to perfect my communication skills, I will never be perfect. But that's okay. It's not okay, however, when I fall back on the same old ineffective language, which is why I try always to study my lines. Sometimes the lines are reflected back at me in the way I'm spoken to. At other times, the lesson is more traditional—I may borrow a phrase from a book or adopt something I've learned in a workshop. In any case, the shift occurs over time with several lapses along the way.

Naturally, before you can begin to study your lines you need to write them down or, at the very least, think them through. As you're composing your lines, remember to include the ones that speak of your passion and your desire to turn the life you're living into the life you want. When you expose your deepest wishes and dreams, people respond. Many will want to help you get there. When Peter Ferrito wanted to create student-leadership work-shops he traveled to Denver to visit with his friend George, who'd always seen the best in Peter. "He encouraged me to do what I always had wanted to do," says Peter. "He suggested that I create a business conducting workshops for youth groups, particularly high school band student-leader teams, student governments, and sports teams. I'd volunteered with a few groups but didn't know how to start a business. The thought of actually making money at this was inconceivable.

"George pushed the envelope when he challenged me to come up with a workshop outline in a day and a half. He told me he'd be introducing me to the directors of the best two bands at a contest in Colorado and would tell them that I conducted leadership and team-building workshops for a living. Within a short time I'd completed the outline and prepared a script with the persuasive language I'd need to sell myself. I used phrases like, 'fitting in while standing out' because once teens can overcome that dilemma, they feel more safe to contribute and help their organizations. Later, I was hired on the spot by both band directors. And Ferrito Education was born."

People generally like to help out when they can, particularly if they can derive a true sense of pride. Think of the times you've helped others and recall the good feeling that comes from simply knowing you helped make someone else happy. Sharing your devotion and enthusiasm toward achieving your dreams will encourage others to do the same. A reciprocal spirit is bound to surface.

As you begin to craft your scripts, don't underestimate the power of editing and cutting some lines altogether. Often, the absence of language says more than what might actually flow from our mouths. Also, don't worry about your speech sounding stilted or artificial. If what you say comes from your heart, your delivery will be as fresh as an opening-night appearance.

experiment

Learn the three-sentence rule. As you meander along the wish-it path you are likely to meet people who express some interest in your goals. Naturally, some will be polite and merely want the facts.

Others may want more detail and will truly be engaged by what you tell them. For each group and everyone in between, you'll want to have a prepared statement, something your listeners can absorb with as little detail as possible. You don't want to omit major facts, yet you mustn't bore your audience either. Whether it's another guest at a party or the CEO of a company you want to work for, you'll want to get the most out of the moments you are given to speak. Whittle your lines down to three and you'll avoid droning on and on. Wrap up your comments by saying something like, "Thank you for listening. Now please tell me what you're doing."

Proceed with truth. Don't confuse studying your lines with being dishonest. Many of us are well schooled in the telling of white lies, and I'm not suggesting that you blurt out words that could be hurtful. On the other hand, don't get stuck in that "zone of nice" in which everything you say must comfort and shield someone else. If we're always nice, we're not necessarily truthful to ourselves, much less to others. Knowing what to say with honesty—and how to say it—is one of the most important ways you can begin to turn what you want into what is yours. For instance, instead of telling someone you have no time and can't be bothered with her project, offer to listen at a later date when you're not so busy. Say something like, "It's a very busy time for me right now, but perhaps you could call me in a few weeks and we can talk for about fifteen minutes." Or, if you have absolutely no interest in connecting with this person, just leave it at how busy you are at this time. Either way, you're letting people know, in a nice way, that your time is valuable.

Practice your lines. Don't be shy about rehearsing your lines. You don't have to stand before a full-length mirror or sit by yourself at the kitchen table. The shower or bath is as safe a place as anywhere to review and hear your lines. Listen to your tone, laugh at your silliness, but give yourself the respect you deserve. Instead of second-guessing yourself, try on some language that implies certainty rather than ambiguity. Resist the temptation to explain, which only dilutes the main point of what you're trying to convey.

Study someone else's lines, too. Do you know someone who communicates well? Sometimes we can borrow the language of others to improve our communication skills. Speaking with economy connotes self-assuredness and focus. Many times the people who use their words sparingly also are the best listeners. We can learn from that as well.

Listen to what you say. Just as we admire the person who chooses her words carefully, we might cringe when we're in the company of someone who talks and talks. We all talk more than we should at one point or another, and, not surprisingly, those are the times when we've ceased listening to ourselves. How many times have you spoken a little more than necessary only to forget what you said? When we listen to ourselves more carefully, we tend to say only what we need to say.

practice

I choose my lines with care and precision because:

1. _____

_____

2. _____

_____

3. _____

_____

When I pin down my words with precision and truth, my wishes and dreams seem:

1. _____

_____

2. _____

_____

3. _____

_____

Studying my lines helps me to be more aware of others because:

1. _____

_____

2. _____

_____

3. _____

_____

affirm

When I study my lines, I give myself permission to think about what I want to say.

When I study my lines, I

_____

_____

~ week 18 ~

Connect

We all act as hinges—fortuitous links between other people.
—Penelope Lively, *Moon Tiger* (1987)

ask

1. Am I comfortable meeting people outside my familiar circle?
2. Do I make an effort to meet new people?
3. Am I willing to connect with others who might want something from me?
4. Do I ask people specific questions about their lives versus the typical "how are you?" inquiries?
5. Do I ever forget about the importance of maintaining connections? Why?
6. Do I think of myself as a good networker?
7. Why do I need to connect with others?

When I first entered the workforce I consistently heard this familiar mantra: "It's not what you know, it's *who* you know." I would nod in agreement and say, "Hm, yes, you're right about that." I was young and didn't know a lot of people outside my small circle of friends and family. So I set out to meet as many people as I could. For many years I focused mostly on the "who," figuring that the "what" wasn't as important. Eventually, though, I discovered that collecting business cards without knowing much about the people handing them out wouldn't get me very far. Besides, I wasn't very good at "working" a room, the proverbial advice given to beginning networkers. I'd always been happiest when I could set down an anchor with one or two people and really learn something—their likes, dislikes, horror stories, dreams, and what they thought of the food.

But the real thrill occurred when I began connecting the people I met with *one another.* I felt like a dealmaker or maybe a matchmaker. Either way, my networking mantra turned into something completely different. Today I am a firm believer that it's not what you know or who you know but *who you can connect with whom.* The networking—hooking up with people who can help me—has become secondary. Instead of asking others what they can do for you, consider how you might do something for them and then just do it. If a colleague has always wanted to speak with your friend who's a juvenile-court judge, see what you can do to make it happen. If a talented new business owner is looking for new clients, ask her for several cards that you can hand out to people who might need her services.

If your life is brimming over with one activity after another, the last thing you want to hear is someone say, "What can you do for me?" People are more likely to remember your thoughtful gesture than your request for something. But don't think you need to give something of yourself each time you meet someone new. Sometimes the best impressions are the ones we leave simply because we asked a few questions and stopped to listen to the answers.

Connecting with others is essential if you want to wish it,

dream it, and do it. Forget for a moment about the specific result you hope for. Forget the favor you're seeking and focus instead on relationships. As you connect with others, those same individuals are connecting with one another. The more people you meet, the more likely you are to experience certain benefits. But don't rely on a schedule. The real advantages of networking aren't necessarily the immediate payoffs that we hope for but rather the delayed miracles that drop into our lives when we least expect them but need them the most. Think of someone you met who months later became the recipient of your kind gesture. Maybe you read, clipped, and sent an article to someone whose new business benefited from the information. Or perhaps something has fallen into your lap because of a connection you made last year. A person you met at a meeting didn't show interest in your services but now has a real need for your time. Have faith in the constant thread that crosses over, winds around, and pulls one person to the next, because ultimately we really are woven together into one powerful and vibrant tapestry.

experiment

Surrender to spontaneity. How many times have you thought about picking up the phone just to hear the sweet voice of someone you love? Or maybe just the sound of a friend who can pack all the essentials into a compact, five-minute, get-up-to-date call? Don't underestimate the sound of your voice, either; imagine the smile that forms on the face of a close friend as she recognizes your voice on the other end of the line. You can also send something through the mail—written in your own hand. The connection you make through a letter, while quiet and unseen, is often felt more vividly than what transpires when face-to-face.

Talk to a stranger. Strangers—not the ones with shifty eyes but those with kindness in their hearts—can open up the unknown in wonderful and vast ways. Some strangers turn into lifelong friends. Others, whom we may never see again, offer generous and sage wisdom . . . on a street corner or in line at the store. Sometimes we are the strangers who kindle the spark for others. And a few inspire us to pursue our dreams. I remember asking novelist Elizabeth Berg at a reading what advice she would give to a nonfiction writer wanting to try her hand at fiction. "It's not as hard as you think," she said. I've never forgotten her words.

Join *something*. Even if you bristle at the thought of joining an organization like Welcome Wagon or Toastmasters—too formal, too many of the same kind of people, too structured—consider the possibility of connecting with just one person on one level at one meeting. It might fuel an idea, prevent you from giving up on an idea too soon, and help you form closer ties to your community.

Volunteer. Who has time, right? Volunteering doesn't mean that you have to head a committee or join a board of directors. You can pick and choose, and you'll always have the right to say, "Sorry, I can't." It's easy to put off volunteering until you reach your goal or when your kids grow up or when you can fit it in. But it's a lot more rewarding to simply take a small slice of your time *now* and devote it to a good cause. Whether you're walking to raise money for breast cancer or reading to your son's first grade, the time and effort you spend will almost always result in at least one connection that could change your life and ultimately help you turn the life you're living into the life you want.

Accept an invitation. When I'm panicked over a deadline or feeling unhinged, it's not easy to accept invitations. I'm not suggesting that you say "yes" each time a friend beckons you to come out and play or that it's not your right to say "no" when you simply have too much to do. Yet, if you decline too often the invitations may cease, and then where are you? Accept an invitation here and there and be grateful for the connection.

practice

For the most part, I connect with people best when I:

1. _____

_____

2. _____

_____

3. _____

_____

It's difficult to connect with others when:

1. _____

_____

2. _____

_____

3. _____

_____

One day I'd like to connect with:

1. _____

_____

2. _____

_____

3. _____

_____

affirm

I realize that my wishes and dreams are bound up in the same yearnings as other dreamers' and that ultimately we can help one another.

When I connect with others, I

_____

_____

~ week 19 ~

Unwrap Your Intuition

It is always with excitement that I wake up in the morning wondering what my intuition will toss up to me, like gifts from the sea. I work with it and rely on it. It's my partner.

—Jonas Salk

ask

1. Do I ever doubt my gut feelings?
2. When have I acted on my intuition?
3. Has my intuition ever failed me?
4. Do I consider intuition a gift?
5. Do I view intuition as a valuable tool in my daily life?
6. How can I hone my intuitive skills?
7. How can my intuition help me turn the life I'm living into the life I want?

Call it a hunch or just an indescribable though visceral sensation. You can't put your finger on it, but you know you're onto something. Perhaps you wait a day before initiating an important conversation, or you postpone a trip because it doesn't feel right to leave home. Whether you act on your hunch or ignore it, that voice inside often wields more influence than even the most persuasive and proven data.

Unfortunately, we do discount that inner voice—our intuition—often when we most need to hear it. The knowledge we can glean from our intuition isn't always based on rational thought, which may explain why we periodically turn down the volume on our inner voice. If you can't explain it, how can it be true? Or perhaps we're afraid of what we might hear. What if you're faced with a significant decision based on what your intuition is telling you?

Relying on your intuition may feel unfamiliar, uncomfortable, and possibly like a total waste of time. After all, many of us were taught to dismiss our intangible insights—our fuzzy understanding of a situation or the negative (or positive) vibes we may get after meeting someone new. It's no surprise that so many people turn away from this gift of self-awareness. Yet, it is this knowledge that can absolutely define who we are and how we cope. If you pay attention to your intuitive voice, you might discover, for example, that a specific issue has more meaning than you'd previously thought. Instead of stressing over a gnawing doubt, you can apply your intuitive skills to work through, not around, the emotion. Your intuition also can be a surprising source of strength, especially in a stressful situation. Susan Page Tillet, an intuitive practitioner, says that intuition is really the essence of who we are *held up to the light*. Instead of tapping in to a dark place, Susan suggests that our intuition opens us up to more clarity, to a place where feelings and emotions are in plain view, not hiding behind a façade or covered up by something painful or untrue.

"A new job opportunity might appear very tempting," says Susan. "But when I check in with my intuition I see that the job is really a distraction rather than a solution. The challenge is to withhold judgment and, instead, use my intuition further to ask what it is I feel is missing in the current situation."

Don't be troubled if you're unable to put what you feel into words. Honing your intuitive skills is a process, and each new discovery is really one part of the cumulative learning that occurs.

experiment

Listen no matter what. Sometimes we don't like what we hear. Whether we're listening to someone else or to ourselves, the information we receive isn't always easy to accept. However, if you do listen with thought and intention you may discover a truth you need to hear. For instance, some people claim that their intuition hasn't always served them well. "My intuition was wrong," they say. Often, though, your intuition may simply be trying to give you information. The data may feel wrong because it takes you by surprise and it may not be what you were hoping for. For example, you might meet someone who, at first, seems like-minded and trustworthy, yet later your intuition sends you a different signal, an uncomfortable message. Listen anyway; sometimes your intuition is the first to know.

Let your intuition save you. Many people who become ill confess that they didn't listen to their intuition. While your intuition will probably not direct you to a precise diagnosis or treatment plan, it can tell you that something just isn't right. Think of heart attack victims who report during their convalescence that, in retrospect, they wish they had listened to their bodies, their intuition. Maybe then they could've taken steps to ward off an attack. It doesn't always seem fathomable that unresolved issues—a difficult childhood, a broken heart, anger, depression, or profound sadness—could create such havoc inside our bodies. Yet, even after suffering a serious illness one's intuition can stay intact. Let it work for you. After all, it could be good for your health.

Give yourself five minutes of peace. When we meditate we enter a realm of tranquility and inner harmony that can actually enhance our abilities to unwrap and then listen to our intuition. And while you may meditate for just five minutes a day, the benefits will last far beyond that short interval. Conjuring up the experience can practically take you there again and again.

Put your intuition on paper. Journaling is a popular and proven method for becoming more self-aware. Just as you might record your dreams in a dream journal to gain insight into and understanding of your nocturnal adventures, consider writing down your intuitive thoughts as well. Buy yourself a decorative journal, something inviting, and commit to using it. Give yourself a week before you make any judgments regarding its utility. Think of your journaling as a dialogue between your intuitive self and your listening self. Journaling also literally gives your intuition a voice. Sometimes that's all it needs to be heard . . . loud and clear.

practice

In the past, I've relied on my intuition to help me:

1. _____

_____

2. _____

_____

3. _____

_____

Lately, I've been having strong, though not always rational, feelings about:

1. _____

_____

2. _____

_____

3. _____

_____

I can do the following three things to hone my intuitive skills:

1. _____

_____

2. _____

_____

3. _____

_____

affirm

I trust my intuition more than fact and physical reality, because it is part of my reality.

When I unwrap my intuition, I

_____

_____

Prosper Wherever You Go

Better to have one good dress than a closetful of mediocre ones.
—Annie Glassman

ask

1. How often do I think about the ways I could make more money?
2. Is my happiness dependent on the amount of money I have?
3. Do I contribute enough to the causes I believe in?
4. Do I balance my checking account on a regular basis?
5. Do the financial pages in the newspaper intimidate me?
6. Am I afraid of becoming financially successful?
7. Have I put my passions on hold as I try to get my finances in order?

When I was in third grade the civil rights leader Martin Luther King, Jr., was assassinated. I knew a darkness had enveloped the country, but from my nine-year-old perspective the fear and uncertainty was much more personal. As the country was mourning the death of a hero, my father's hardware store was burning to the ground as the streets of Washington, D.C. erupted with civil unrest. Like a lot of children whose parents are immersed in catastrophe, I tried to stay out of the way. Throughout the following weeks and beyond I heard a lot about the roof over our heads. "Financial ruin" was a hazy concept for me. "Having a roof over our head," however, was a phrase that I could understand. My parents didn't lose their home, but we did experience tremendous loss. To this day I am grateful for the roof over my head. I don't remember being scared about the possibility of leaving our home, but my understanding of and appreciation for shelter was changed forever.

My childhood—particularly my family's experience in 1968—has a lot of bearing on the way I think about money. I don't like to be in debt. I am always happy to have a warm and comfortable place to call home. And, like other women, sometimes I worry that despite hard work and sensible planning, I might end up without shelter. I'm beginning to believe, though, that my feelings and attitudes about money have to change. When I worry too much about the source of my abundance, I prevent it from flowing into my life. That's why I've decided to prosper wherever I go.

You don't have to have loads of money to prosper. Nor do you need a pot of gold at every turn on your journey to wish, dream, and do. But it is essential to develop a sense of abundance—for your work, for yourself, and for others—in order to turn the life you're living into the life you want. Spend happily but be sensible, avoid debt when you can, and make a habit of putting money away every month. It's more than simply focusing on—and appreciating—what you have. It's about holding the world's possibilities with open palms and embracing an attitude that engenders a sense of bounty.

Too often, though, we turn away from our ability to prosper. We become slaves to our financial security and find ourselves in a constant state of worry. Pursuing a passion begins to feel trivial and unnecessary, almost undeserving. It is at this point that our financial *insecurities* take over and block our abilities to achieve our dreams. Andrea Ellis Oppenheim, a financial adviser with Merrill Lynch, says, "Deprivation is not the goal." Andrea instructs her clients to ask themselves about their values. "It doesn't matter how much or how little money someone has," she says. "The question is: Are your values in line with your daily movements? For example, if you tell someone you want to spend more time with your kids, reconsider all the hours you spend running from one activity to another. People who work so hard to keep up might do better to stay home once in a while and make soup or cookies with their kids." Using Andrea's suggestion, look at a typical week and think about how your daily movements and what you spend align with what's really important in your life.

experiment

Pay the most important bill of all. Wouldn't it be easier to save if we all received a bill every month for *ourselves*? That's right. Every month you'd get an invoice reminding you to put something into your financial-health account. Of course, that's not going to happen, but you can shift around your priorities and pay yourself first—for retirement, reserves for an emergency expense, start-up money for a new business, and peace of mind. Aren't you worth it?

Make a friend at your bank. Nina is my favorite banker. She always waves when I enter the bank, and when she's not on the phone or helping a customer, I stop by her desk to say hello. I even got to schmooze with Nina at the airport a few years ago as we both waited to board a flight to Baltimore. But what I appreciate the most is that Nina is willing to untangle my statements and help me make sense of what I have. She's a safety net for me. Find a safety net at your local bank. It'll help you bring things under control.

Live it up. You don't have to spend thousands—or even hundreds—to infuse a little luxury into your life. Besides, if you deprive yourself too often, you're more likely to indulge in self-pity and focus too much on what you don't have. Also, depriving yourself of things that money can buy is not unlike denying yourself a sweet (or salty) treat when you're watching your weight. If you do that too much, a binge could be right around the corner. And just as an eating binge is bad for your health, too many spending sprees can harm your financial well-being. Once in a while, though, don't just smell the roses, buy yourself a dozen.

Share your dollars and sense. One of the easiest ways to prosper is to share your wealth, whether it's your money or your expertise. All of us have value, and as the saying goes, time is money. When you volunteer your time, you're sharing a piece of yourself, your value. If you write a check, you can see for yourself that you have enough to share. This helps to diffuse the anxiety and worry about money, and this, of course, leads to a more abundant state of mind.

Scan the financial pages. Just because you're not a "numbers" person doesn't mean you can't pick up a little information about the economy. Being familiar with the big picture will help you understand it. Andrea, the financial adviser, suggests a ten-minute commitment every day. "Read the business section of your local paper or browse through a financial web site," she says. "The money and investing section on the front page of *The Wall Street Journal* is a great place to start." If the numbers and graphs scare you, stick with the text. Remember that it's just words.

Start a cash stash. At the end of the day, empty all your change into a jar. I keep two in the cupboard, one for each of my children. When the jars are full I take them to the bank and make a deposit. It feels great, and I rarely miss the money.

practice

In the past, I've been afraid to manage my money because:

1. _____

_____

2. _____

_____

3. _____

_____

I would feel more prosperous if I could:

1. _____

_____

2. _____

_____

3. _____

_____

I will take one or more of the following steps this week toward winning my financial freedom and infusing more prosperity into my life:

1. _____

   _____

2. _____

   _____

3. _____

   _____

affirm

When I prosper wherever I go, I let go of the guilt that, before, prevented me from inviting abundance into my life.

When I prosper wherever I go, I

_____

_____

~ week 21 ~

Outgrow Your Shell

My favorite thing to do is to go where I've never been.

—Diane Arbus, *Diane Arbus* (1972)

ask

1. Do I need a lot of time to absorb certain changes?
2. Can I grow through good times and bad?
3. Am I able to talk comfortably with others when I experience personal growth?
4. What kind of support do I have to help me move through the changes ahead?
5. Am I willing to take certain risks that ultimately will help me grow?
6. Can I let go of old habits so that inner growth is possible?
7. Do I ever sabotage my dreams because I am resistant to change?

Let's take a look at the behavior of the hermit crab, a creature born without its protective covering. To safeguard its soft abdomen, the hermit crab looks for an empty shell and makes it its home. When the crab outgrows the shell, it looks for another to provide shelter. Its growth requires the crab to find new digs on a regular basis. What if we were forced to move each time we grew? Sometimes we deny ourselves the chance to grow because we don't like change, so we end up wearing the same shell. If you want to wish, dream, and do, you must be willing to outgrow your shell. Maybe you need to further your education and enroll in school. Or perhaps you should consider a different job that will force you to step out of your comfort zone.

Some people love change. Others will tell you they'd rather undergo a root canal then make a major change. In some cases, resisting change is like ignoring the elephant in your living room. Other opportunities for growth are more subtle. Big or insignificant, change can make us ambivalent. We rock back and forth between familiarity and the unknown. And then there's what you leave behind—a part of yourself, a slice of history, a memory. Indeed, how can a comfortable past compete with an uncertain future?

Often what keeps us from embracing change is our unrealistic belief that we can actually hold on to the here and now. We can hold on to it, but just for as long as it lasts. Then it's a memory, a wonderful cherished memory. To truly turn the life we're living into the life we want, we must loosen our grip on the status quo. Working at something outside your area of expertise could complement rather than distract from your efforts. If you've always worked alone, consider collaborating on one project with a partner. Or, if you've always worked for other people but yearn to be your own boss, try consulting or freelancing. See how you like it before you decide it's not for you. Just because things change doesn't mean that we can't manage.

Each time I encounter adversity, I know that change and growth is inevitable. It is this knowledge that helps me move through the challenge. I know I will get *something* from the struggle. If we remain static through difficulties, we generally don't learn very much. As you stretch and grow through each experience, be assured that the changes before you will make you stronger, wiser, and clearer about your life. As dreamers and doers, we are always in the process of *becoming*.

experiment

Allow yourself to say good-bye. Often, a change leaves sadness in its wake. It's painful to think about the loss of something even when there's been a gain. Yet, it's a necessary step toward growth. People who move frequently, for example, are accustomed to managing a morass of emotions ranging from excitement and anticipation to melancholy and anxiety. Generally, these people experience personal growth that might not have occurred had they stayed put. Allow yourself to mourn so that the growth is authentic and unencumbered by unresolved sorrow.

Bring your growth out into the open. Sometimes we experience and put into practice a change, but we keep it to ourselves. Maybe you've discovered an easier way to accomplish a specific task, but you don't trust the process because it's not what you're used to. As a result, you play down your discovery. Or it seems too easy, as if a streamlined version can't possibly be as good as the more difficult and complex model. Bring your change and the ensuing growth out in the open. You've given birth to something, so now take care of it and let it grow even more. For example, if you've made a healthy improvement to your lifestyle, let people know, and do what you need to do to maintain the benefits.

Remember past triumphs. When you're faced with a particularly daunting challenge, one that signals a forthcoming and dramatic change, imagine your past triumphs over adversity. Remind yourself of the strength you had then, and put that power to use today. If you've lost some business, recall a time when your income took a dive and the steps you took to get through. Put those old strategies back in place, making adjustments as necessary.

practice

Sometimes change is painful for me because:

1. _____

_____

2. _____

_____

3. _____

_____

When I'm resistant to change, I feel:

1. _____

_____

2. _____

_____

3. _____

_____

Here are some areas in which I'd like to grow:

1. _____

_____

2. _____

_____

3. _____

_____

affirm

Although I might mourn what I leave behind, I am hopeful, even certain, that what I subsequently discover will enhance my journey.

When I outgrow my shell, I

_____

_____

~ week 22 ~

Give Something Back

If we all tried to make other people's paths easy, our own feet would have a smooth even place to walk on.

—Myrtle Reed, *A Weaver of Dreams* (1911)

ask

1. What do I love doing that would benefit others?
2. How much time can I commit to volunteer work?
3. Can I give something back without expecting a reward or public recognition?
4. How does the community add to the quality of my life?
5. Am I comfortable spending time with strangers?
6. Is it important to me to make a difference in someone else's life, someone I don't know?
7. What kind of service can I provide that is aligned with my dreams?

Judith runs a hotel in downtown Chicago. A few years ago, she "adopted" Coles Elementary, a school that serves minority students, most of whom receive public aid. Judith, along with other hotel employees, regularly visit the school, where they read or help with art projects. Seasonally, the hotel lobby features a "mitten tree," where hats, scarves, and mittens have been collected for more than two hundred children. The staff also raises funds for the school through bake sales, Valentine candy sales, and contributions. To date, more than twelve thousand dollars has been donated for academic materials, along with used computers, telephones, and other equipment.

"If you're lucky enough to be born into a family and environment where you have what you need both physically and spiritually, isn't it your responsibility to help those who may not have had those advantages?" says Judith. "Plus, we've been working with the same classrooms, so we're really getting to know each other. It's just the right thing to do."

Opportunities to serve are absolutely endless. Log on to a site such as www.volunteermatch.org and you'll find literally thousands of ways that you can become a volunteer. Jay Backstrand, president of VolunteerMatch, believes that giving back to the community ultimately helps the giver as much as the recipient. "The feeling of personal reward and fulfillment that comes from the simple act of volunteering is overwhelmingly powerful. It helps each of us tap in to a sense of community and perspective that builds the confidence we need to make our own dreams come true. It also makes us more knowledgeable about the people who make up our communities—those in need of help and those who choose to help. Witnessing this give-and-take inspires us to take control of our own lives, our dreams," he says.

It's not surprising that when people are asked about their volunteer work they often express gratitude for having had the chance to help others. It makes us feel good when we can make a positive difference in someone's life. It gives us a sense of purpose and connection with humanity. Giving something back also enables us to make a lasting impression in a world where individual contributions aren't always recognized or appreciated. Clearly, some projects reap excellent publicity, and that's part of the game in a capitalist society. Still, ask most people how they feel after devoting their time to a worthy cause and you'll probably notice a look of hope, enthusiasm, and gratitude all wrapped into one.

Before you sign up to volunteer you need to know two things: (1) the amount of time you're willing to spend on a project and (2) what really, truly moves you. If you don't like blood and can't stand seeing someone in pain, then for goodness' sake stay away from hospitals. If you can speak English and Spanish and you're a software whiz, seek out an opportunity as a bilingual computer instructor. If you love to read and want to share the joy of books, tutor for a literacy council. The list goes on and on. Surprisingly, even those of us who can't imagine adding one more activity to our lives seem to thrive when we carve out a little time to serve.

experiment

Develop your community ties. In my first book, *Will This Place Ever Feel Like Home? Simple Advice for Settling in After You Move,* I suggest that if you've recently moved, you consider volunteer work as a way to connect with your new community. But even if you've lived in the same place for years you may not really feel connected to anything. When you become involved in your community you establish roots. You also become known by other people who might want to help you wish, dream, and do. For instance, if you helped produce the school play, another parent volunteer who admired your commitment and interest may offer you assistance in the future.

Do something good for your health. Scientists have found that people who volunteer often enjoy better health through the formation of social support networks. Researchers believe that people with increased social contacts have lower premature death rates, less heart disease, and fewer health risk factors. That alone should be enough reason to want to give something back.

Do what you love. When you give something back—something you love—you share the best part of who you are. It doesn't even feel like giving. It's as natural as breathing. When you give with passion, your enthusiasm is infectious. People can't help but be influenced by your energy. Your attention also conveys an important message: You value someone else's life. Helping people feel valued is one of life's most precious gifts. It's not wrapped in a box with a bow, but it stands tall and its smile is immense.

Make an indelible impact. One of the best ways to make an indelible mark is to volunteer. Teaching someone to read, giving parents of ill children a break, serving on a committee at your child's school, or collecting trash along the highway are all noble ways to affect your environment and the people who live there. That your good deed goes unnoticed by most of the world does not diminish for a minute your contribution.

practice

Other people might benefit from my abilities to:

1. _____

   _____

2. _____

   _____

3. _____

_____

In the past, I postponed volunteering because:

1. _____

_____

2. _____

_____

3. _____

_____

I have always wanted to help others by:

1. _____

_____

2. _____

_____

3. _____

_____

affirm

When I serve my community, even in the smallest way, I become more connected with my surroundings.

When I give something back, I feel

_____

_____

Sit with Your Disappointment

*Discouragement seizes us only when we can no
longer rely on chance.*
—George Sand, *Handsome Lawrence* (1872)

ask

1. In general, are my expectations realistic?
2. Do I express my expectations clearly?
3. Am I willing to accept people for who they are rather than what I expect them to be?
4. Do I hold other people responsible for what happens in my life?
5. When do I feel disappointed in myself?
6. How did I handle a recent disappointment?
7. How can I learn from my disappointments?

Sitting with your disappointment is a little like tending to a close friend who's trying to get through a difficult time. Fragile and wounded, she might simply need companionship. You may not say much; the conversation may focus on the weather or your new pair of shoes. But your presence will speak volumes. Eventually, you will help your friend emerge from the episode and may then accompany her toward hope and other possibilities.

Like your friend who, hopefully, will slowly separate from the acute pain of her situation, you too must break away from your disappointments to make room for new joys and discoveries. At first, some disappointments can absolutely immobilize us. We get sucked into the hurt and may even begin to anticipate bad things happening. Instead of seeing an opening, we feel confined and become pessimistic. We wash our language in disappointment and gloomy anticipation. Instead of saying, "I've got to do this differently next time," you say, "This always happens to me." Rather than reevaluate a relationship, you put the onus on others who simply can't be what you need them to be: "She does this every time."

To move away from your disappointment you must try to understand its origins and become comfortable with the initial bad feelings that arise when life doesn't go as planned or when people behave in ways that surprise and puzzle you. I don't believe the goal is never to be disappointed. Just as our hearts and souls draw us toward the goodness of others, we're still at times attracted to human qualities that often prove harmful. Unfortunately, we are not immune to spiritual injury, though a deeper awareness of how and why we react the way we do can lessen our pain. Pushing these feelings into a corner may clear the moment, but later, especially if you experience a similar setback, the feelings of disillusionment and even sorrow will return swiftly.

Pay close attention to the people and situations associated with your disappointments. Then, instead of dwelling on someone else's shortcomings, examine your expectations and the strategies you might use the next time around.

Learning from your experiences—how they will help and motivate—will also place you on a path that is future oriented. If you're passed over for a coveted job, think about what you might do differently at your next interview rather than obsess about whom might have gotten that job. If you pestered someone because you tried too hard, figure out how you can change your approach. If you sit with your disappointment for too long, you'll remain in the past. Wishing and dreaming will take on a sense of lethargy and your labor of love will turn to pure drudgery. Not surprisingly, you might also become angry and trapped in a spiral of self-sabotaging behaviors. By asking yourself, "What has this taught me? What are the lessons here?" your pain will slowly dissolve and be replaced by confidence and a new resolve.

experiment

Temper your expectations. Calibrate your expectations of others and of yourself. Often, we expect others to help us simply because we believe they should. Perhaps they've promised their support, but due to unforeseen circumstances cannot provide any help after all; or they've agreed to share the name of an influential contact but when you ask for the person's number you learn that the connection is more tenuous than you'd originally thought. Unfortunately, events and circumstances often preclude us from doing what we say we can do to lend support. If someone's life is interrupted by tragedy, for instance, you may not get the support that was offered four months earlier. We must budget for—and anticipate—the times when our expectations are not met.

Make a distinction between constructive and destructive criticism. When you set your wishes and dreams out into the world, you open yourself up for commentary. From the strangest of strangers to siblings and parents who've known you forever, people will regale you with their points of view—both good and bad.

Separating the useful criticism from the words that can damage or destroy is absolutely critical for your wishes and dreams to survive. I am always stunned when I hear of someone who has questioned the validity of a friend's dream. Some people are simply better at deconstructing creativity, while others are intent upon helping it grow and flourish. Know the difference between constructive and destructive criticism and I can practically guarantee that you will learn how to detach yourself gracefully from the disappointment and move on to your next important step. If the criticism propels you forward, it's constructive. If it sounds like a put-down, it's destructive and should be disregarded.

Get perspective. We'd all be better off if we could look into the future to see how a particular disappointment may possibly be played out. Ten years from now, will this experience still be disappointing? Will anyone—other than you—still remember? If not, how much time and energy should you invest in mourning what didn't occur or what you didn't get?

practice

I get disappointed when:

1. _____

_____

2. _____

_____

3. _____

_____

Sometimes I disappoint myself when I:

1. _____

_____

2. _____

_____

3. _____

_____

I learn from my disappointments when I:

1. _____

_____

2. _____

_____

3. _____

_____

affirm

My ability to learn from each setback diminishes the potency of subsequent disappointments.

When I sit with my disappointment, I

_____

_____

~ week 24 ~

Pick Your Heroes Carefully

You can't ever be really free if you admire somebody too much.
—Tove Jansson, *Tales from Moominvalley* (1963)

ask

1. What does *hero* mean to me?
2. Who in my life has helped me to grow and deepen my character?
3. Who are some unlikely heroes in my past, people who weren't necessarily larger than life but nevertheless made a difference in my life?
4. Am I attracted to unconventional heroes? Why? Who are they?
5. How tolerant am I of the human frailties that afflict us all, including my heroes?
6. Have my heroes ever let me down?
7. Do I even need heroes in my life?

Who are your heroes? Are they trailblazers and pioneers with familiar names and impressive biographies? Perhaps your heroes live quieter lives, ones that beget anonymity and modesty. Your heroes might even be more fleeting—a stranger who hands you your wallet when it's fallen to the ground, the neighbor whose sharp eye and compassionate instincts keep your child out of the path of an oncoming car, even the dinner guest who, in spite of a kitchen catastrophe, assures you that all is well and that carryout is just thirty minutes away.

Selecting a hero is a little like sharing a secret. Before you set your secret free, you must know in your heart that it will be kept in confidence. Similarly, you must ask yourself if your heroes can realistically live up to your expectations. Occasional disappointments are to be expected. Everyone—heroes included—experience lapses in judgment and stumble over adversity in ways that, in hindsight, may have been avoided. Yet, if our heroes repeatedly disappoint us, we lose faith and may even feel betrayed.

Throughout history our heroes have sought to improve conditions for sometimes just a few or in some cases thousands. Some lived in obscurity; others have become renowned for their deeds, documented for the world to see. Regardless of their notoriety or quiet reserve, our heroes keep our faith alive, which helps to make wishing, dreaming, and doing a hopeful and promising endeavor. For example, if we're feeling particularly vulnerable or apprehensive about the future, a hero's example can put things into perspective. Think of the former welfare mothers who've turned their lives around because of their pure hope and drive. Imagine the child who's bullied for years yet grows up to be a teacher who shows the next generation how to treat people with kindness.

We can admire, praise, and honor their decency, but in the end it is what we do with our own lives that matters most. Whether our role models inspire us to be courageous, kind, or persistent, we must be certain that their values align with our own. Also, contrary to what we've come to believe, pedestals are not necessarily the best place for our heroes to exist. Holding our heroes in our hearts and souls will bring their gifts closer to where we stand so that we, too, can be heroes. Your admiration of Eleanor Roosevelt or the woman down the street can become the fuel you need to wish, dream, and do. And be absolutely clear on one thing: Don't worry if your heroes enjoy an obscure status. Consider the remarks of Margaret Mead found in a 1992 issue of *The Utne Reader:* "A small group of thoughtful people could change the world. Indeed, it's the only thing that ever has."

experiment

Go back in time. Go to the library or your local bookstore and select a few biographies of heroes. You'll find familiar names, but you'll also read about astonishing people whose names you might not recognize but whose deeds will resonate with your desires to wish, dream, and do.

Read the comics. Alex Ross, a well-known comic-book creator, has been learning from colorful superheroes for most of his life. "Superheroes aren't heroes because they're strong," he says, "they're heroes because they perform acts that look beyond themselves." Take a look at some of Alex's work or grab a comic book at the drugstore while you're waiting for a prescription and take some inspiration from these fictional icons who share some of the same human frailties and flaws as we experience.

Write your hero a letter. Composing a letter to your hero—whether you send it or not—may lead to some discoveries about yourself. A letter to your hero might include a list of the characteristics you admire or even questions you wish you could ask if given the chance. You could even describe an episode during which your hero's example helped you get through a difficult situation.

Pluck a name from obscurity. In most cases, the real heroes are the people whose names we'll probably never know. A heroic act might simply be the years that someone puts into a less than satisfactory job in order to put food on the family dinner table or the cousin who quits her job to take care of her ailing parent. Can you think of someone whose perseverance and selfless actions improved someone else's life? Have you read about a hometown hero whose small contribution enhanced the lives of others? Think of ways you can apply the lessons of everyday heroes to your life.

practice

My heroes are:

1. _____

_____

2. _____

_____

3. _____

_____

They've taught me about:

1. _____

_____

2. _____

_____

3. _____

_____

Their heroic qualities inspire me to:

1. _____

_____

2. _____

_____

3. _____

_____

affirm

It is not always the loudest and strongest who deserve admiration but rather those whose service and actions occur with little fanfare and often with no warning.

When I pick my heroes carefully, I

_____

_____

Celebrate New Year's Every Day

Our being is subject to all the chances of life. There are so many things we are capable of, that we could be or do. The potentialities are so great that we never, any of us, are more than one-fourth fulfilled.

—Katherine Anne Porter interview in
Writers at Work, Second Series (1963),
edited by George Plimpton

ask

1. How often do I make the same resolutions?
2. Can I honestly manage to do something tomorrow that seems impossible today?
3. Does starting over mean I'm accountable all over again?
4. Isn't starting over another way of procrastinating what I really need to do?
5. Do I associate starting over with something new and different?
6. Do I even believe in resolutions?
7. Is it difficult for me to take the first step necessary to turn the life I'm living into the life I want?

*H*ave you ever wanted to scramble the calendar so that you could rewrite your resolutions? Are you discovering that it's easier—and makes more sense—to set realistic goals rather than implement big, sweeping changes in a short period of time? We're pretty good at planning out a strategy for self-improvement, particularly on the first day of the year. Sustaining those challenges, however, is the real challenge. Still, unlike any other day, New Year's seems to offer fresh promise and possibility simply because it's what we've come to believe. Why not celebrate second chances and your own potential each day as if the New Year were spread out before you?

Celebrating New Year's every day doesn't mean you have to bring out the champagne and make a toast to peace and prosperity (though that's not such a bad idea—at least the peace and prosperity part). Instead of obsessing over broken resolutions, redirect that energy by celebrating your right to start again. The possibilities—indeed, your future—belong to you. Where we are in life— our responsibilities, ages, skills—often dictate how much we can accomplish at any given time. I've always wanted to volunteer at a women's shelter, but for now I try to give in other ways. Friends tell me they'd like to start new businesses, go back to school, and give back to the community. For some, the time is now. For others, a dream might be temporarily put aside. Instead of relegating your possibilities to one day of the year, spread them out like a deck of cards so that you can see exactly what you're holding in your hands.

experiment

Space your resolutions. Saving up all your resolutions for one night of the year is a huge burden. Consider making resolutions throughout the year with the understanding that you'll do the best you can over the course of 365 days. Isn't that more realistic?

Celebrate your milestones. Celebrate your milestones no matter what. If you made a commitment last spring that's finally coming to fruition today, then by all means blow your own horn and have a party. Of course, you can do this by yourself at the kitchen table or invite a few good friends to help you savor your sweet victory.

Start over. When you start over you give yourself the opportunity to cast off the ideas and tactics that haven't advanced you closer to your goals. Sometimes it's hard to let go of something so familiar. On the other hand, it can be exhilarating to clear your plate so that you can make room for something better.

practice

In the past, I've held on to believing that I'd always:

1. _____

_____

2. _____

_____

3. _____

_____

Instead of waiting for midnight on December 31, I'm going to resolve right now to:

1. _____

_____

2. _____

_____

3. _____

_____

I will celebrate my achievements by:

1. _____

_____

2. _____

_____

3. _____

_____

affirm

I can always make a fresh start and I am always on the cusp of something wonderful.

When I celebrate New Year's every day, I

_____

_____

~ week 26 ~

Support Another Dreamer

Those whom we support hold us up in life.
—Marie von Ebner-Eschenbach, *Aphorisms* (1893)

ask

1. Do I generally support others in their pursuit of dreams?
2. Can I help others when I'm so busy trying to hold it together for myself?
3. Do I expect anything in return when I support others?
4. Do I understand the difference between being nice and being supportive?
5. Do other dream catchers support me? Does that matter to me?
6. How can I offer support?
7. How can helping others make it easier for me to shepherd my wishes and dreams?

If you can assist and encourage others to achieve their dreams amid your pursuit, you may uncover some of your previously hidden assets. Sometimes we pass on advice or an attitude that, until we can articulate it, is precisely what we've been seeking for ourselves. And though your intentions are to merely help others you will undoubtedly be on the receiving end as well. For example, you might advise a friend to vigorously promote her business even if it feels uncomfortable to her. Later, you might heed your own advice. After all, what we tell others to do is usually what we need to do for ourselves.

Not everyone will want your help. Some will feel threatened and may even consider your gesture an intrusion. Indeed, a few may question your sincerity. Respect their points of view and maintain your role as supporter. In fact, sometimes it's more appropriate to do nothing at all. Just because someone doesn't take your advice or follow in your footsteps doesn't necessarily mean that she doesn't appreciate your support or that your guidance isn't sound. You never know when or where a seed might take root.

As you think about ways you might reach out to others pursuing their dreams, ask yourself what you can do to help. Make sure you understand why your support matters and always try to be honest—with others, but especially with yourself—about your motivation even if it means that, yes, you hope the help may one day be reciprocated. Finally, be careful to extend your support to people who won't drain your reserves.

It's important to garner support from our friends, but others can provide a level of encouragement as well. Sometimes we help other people simply because we can, not for what the exchange may bring in the form of friendship. Certainly, many friendships are the result of one person reaching out to another, but it is possible to support others without the expectation that a long-term relationship will emerge. If you keep an open mind and heart and remain true to yourself and your goals, you will know when and how to support another dreamer. This will help you sustain the energy and drive you need to catch your dreams as well. For example, you can offer to mentor someone without becoming her friend. Or you might invite a colleague to a meeting where she can meet prospective clients without keeping you from doing what you need to do.

In either case, use your time wisely and be clear with yourself on how much you can reasonably invest in someone else's dreams.

experiment

Check in. It's always nice to unexpectedly hear from a supporter. "How's it going?" may be just what's necessary for someone to step up her efforts to wish, dream, and do. You don't have to adhere to a regular schedule for checking in, though you may have a lot of catching up to do if your calls are spread too far apart. Often, we dreamers come to expect these calls, which frequently spur us on.

Launch a Wish It Group. One of the best ways to stay focused is to seek out others who are as enthusiastic and committed to their dreams as you are. Consider launching a Wish It Group. You can find people by word of mouth or even through an ad placed in your local paper. Professional groups are also a fruitful resource for finding like-minded dreamcatchers. In addition to providing support, your "advisers" can offer guidance on a variety of issues and circumstances. Sometimes all you need is another perspective to gain a little clarity. An initial meeting might include some discussion on mutual goals, meeting dates and places, and ground rules for the team. Many teams like this succeed because each person is dedicated to helping the other members inch closer to their wishes and dreams through the exchange of ideas, contacts, and resources. In a writing group, for example, members take turns reviewing one another's manuscripts. Each person receives equal amounts of support because the meetings are structured to ensure that outcome. (Read more about starting a Wish It Group in "One More Thought," page 267.)

Start a clipping service. I'm always so touched when a friend forwards an article of interest to me. Sometimes it's folded up inside a greeting card or covered by a Post-it with a short note. You can send other dreamers pieces of information that may otherwise never cross their desks. Even if you send something only once or twice a year, your efforts will be remembered and appreciated.

Celebrate! Cheer for your fellow dreamers. Help them celebrate all their triumphs—big and small. If a pal has shed two pounds in her efforts to lose thirty, shower her with congratulations. If a colleague has nailed her first big client, let her know how happy you are by sending a festive bouquet of flowers or balloons.

Bite your tongue. When you're asked for an opinion or feel the urge to state your mind, speak with compassion. Frame your language with questions like "How will that strategy move you closer to your goal?" or "Has that been useful in the past?" Remember to separate your inner critic from the person seeking your support, and try to focus on what someone is doing right.

practice

In the past, I've received support when others have:

1. _____

_____

2. _____

_____

3. _____

_____

I can offer my help to the following people:

1. _____

_____

2. _____

_____

3. _____

_____

When I support others, I feel:

1. _____

_____

2. _____

_____

3. _____

_____

affirm

I give to others what I have received so that I can make more room for the good that is ahead.

When I support another dreamer, I

_____

_____

Know the Answer to "Who Do You Think You Are?"

*Self-trust, we know, is the first secret of suc-
cess.*
—Lady Wilde, "Miss Martineau," *Notes on Men,
Women, and Books* (1891)

ask

1. Who *do* I think I am anyway?
2. When I'm feeling doubtful, how do I respond to this question?
3. When I'm confident, how do I respond to this question?
4. In what ways do I seek the approval of others?
5. How important is their approval?
6. How do I respond when I feel that others are judging me?
7. Are my wishes and dreams unreasonable?

As you progress on your journey you will undoubtedly encounter subtle and often unexpected resistance. Someone you know—or even a stranger—will question your motives. You might not actually hear the words, but you will know instinctively that your efforts are being judged. If a person sees you living a life that doesn't match her model, she may feel threatened and offer criticism instead of support. You may be asked, for example, exactly how long you've been working on your dream. Or perhaps you'll be grilled on whom you know, implying that your efforts and any subsequent success are tied to someone who's more powerful and influential than you.

When we doubt ourselves, we're really questioning our worthiness. In fact, the response you provide to "Who do you think you are?" is inexorably linked to your belief in yourself. For example, if you're an unpublished writer and someone asks what you do, simply say, "I'm a writer." Don't apologize and don't confuse some sort of institutional recognition for what you are trying to become. Too often people mistake self-confidence for self-importance, but usually these are the same critics who aren't sure of *themselves.*

experiment

Take a true/false test. Remember taking true/false tests in school? They were deceptive in their simplicity. True, false, true, true, false, false. Sometimes, though, these exams turned out to be more challenging than writing an essay. Similarly, in life we forget how difficult and complicated the truth can be. Yet, once you commit to living a truthful life, it becomes easier to distinguish between what's true and what's false. Just don't be afraid of the truth. Doubt is more prevalent in our lives when we have trouble accepting the truth. The more you accept your truths, the less you will be paralyzed by self-doubt.

Write down who you are. Write yourself a note and tape it to your bathroom mirror: *Mirror, mirror, on the wall, you're the greatest of them all.* Or, just as you might keep a gratitude journal, consider writing down the answer to "Who do you think you are?" Be sure to date your entries so that you can reread and chart your progress.

Promote yourself. Self-promotion is a learned art, and once you've mastered the do's and don'ts, it's as natural as stating your name. Leadership coach Peggy Klaus, who teaches a Bragging Rites and Wrongs workshop, believes that people must learn to talk about themselves, their ideas, and their accomplishments with pride, conviction, and a sense of delight. "Job interviews, promotions, bonuses, and referrals—just to name a few critical career builders—are determined not just by your performance but how you tell the story," Klaus, author of *Brag! The Art of Tooting Your Own Horn Without Blowing It*, says. "If you can't do it well, or worse, won't do it because you are too afraid of being labeled a braggart, you are doing yourself a huge disservice."

Many of us, however, were never taught how to effectively promote ourselves. You must be willing to take credit for your accomplishments. You will always be your own best advocate.

Be yourself. When we act fraudulently, we trip all over ourselves. Nothing comes naturally. When we're ourselves, we can relax more and worry less. Answering the question, "Who do you think you are?" becomes practically effortless.

practice

I doubt myself when:

1. _____

_____

2. _____

_____

3. _____
_____

When I'm wishing and dreaming, I worry that:

1. _____
_____

2. _____
_____

3. _____
_____

I will worry less about outcomes if I can:

1. _____
_____

2. _____
_____

3. _____
_____

affirm

Uncertainty does not reflect fear or doubt but rather my freedom to consider all the wonderful possibilities of who I might become.

When I know the answer to "Who do you think you are?" I

_____
_____

Persevere in Spite of Obstacles and Other Perils

The world doesn't come to the clever folks, it comes to the stubborn, obstinate, one-idea-at-a-time people.
—Mary Roberts Rinehart, "The Family Friend,"
Affinities (1920)

ask

1. Do I tend to give up easily when faced with a seemingly insurmountable hurdle?
2. Do I devote enough time and energy toward minimizing the obstacles in my life?
3. Am I ever afraid that by eliminating an obstacle I will hurt someone's feelings?
4. Will establishing boundaries help me to persevere in spite of the obstacles that threaten to undermine my success?
5. Why are boundaries so important anyway?
6. Can I accept the notion that many obstacles are, indeed, unfair yet resolve to do something about them anyway?
7. Do I ever create my own obstacles? Why?

You'll always be faced with obstacles. Life is funny that way: Just when things are running smoothly, something or someone comes along to throw your equilibrium out of whack. Obstacles can strengthen your resolve. Obstacles can cause you to lose faith. Either way, just because you can't prevent obstacles doesn't mean you can't overcome or sidestep them. It will take work and, most of all, patience. By strategically distancing yourself from certain barriers, you are more likely to minimize—or at least be prepared for—the situations that stand in the way of your happiness and success.

Sometimes our obstacles are securely moored and we must do our best to work around them. Other hurdles, though, are more shifty and maintain an annoying two-feet-behind-us presence. Regardless of how your obstacles manifest themselves, you must be committed to preserving your sense of self. You can try to wait for your obstacles to go away all by themselves, but chances are that without your interference these barriers—those pesky tyrannies that prevent us from moving forward—to your success are unlikely to simply disappear. For example, if your computer acts up each time you go online, do what's necessary to remedy the situation. If a medical condition arises in the middle of a busy time at work, discuss the situation with your boss and/or colleagues so that projects and schedules can be maintained. Think of yourself as a hired troubleshooter, the consultant who's brought in to restore and maintain order. Don't expect the process to be a comfortable one. This is going to be hard work. But you'll become strong and experience a new sense of peace as your obstacles lose their power.

experiment

Surrender . . . sometimes. Understand and accept the fact that you will lose some battles. But this is not defeat. If you know this from the start, you'll be easier on yourself and you'll know when to move on. Don't think of an obstacle as a big wall enclosing you; it's a rock or a felled tree in your way, that's all.

Take one step at a time. Break down your obstacles one piece at a time. This way, instead of trying to handle something huge and insurmountable, you focus on smaller, more manageable tasks. For example, if you're developing a promotional strategy for your new business—from a new web site to stationery and business cards—first create a separate file for each piece of the plan and then assign start and finish dates for each part.

Share your pain. Talk to others who can empathize with your feelings. Don't be afraid to ask for advice, and understand that no one is immune to the spontaneous and unsettling nature of roadblocks. You're likely to glean some wisdom that you'd otherwise not hear. Tell yourself, "I will learn something from this," and then do so. Turn your learning experience into "idea power" that will be the fuel you'll need for the next time around.

Compare and contrast. As you wrestle with your obstacles consider friends, coworkers, and anyone else who might have encountered similar circumstances. Ask yourself these questions: (I) How did someone else handle a particularly difficult situation? (2) How do my circumstances compare with those of others? and (3) What can I do now? You'd be amazed at how much strength you can derive from the way someone else handles adversity.

practice

I am often faced with the following obstacles:

1. _____
   _____

2. _____
   _____

3. _____
   _____

Sometimes I create my own obstacles when I:

1. _____
   _____

2. _____
   _____

3. _____
   _____

I am willing to learn from my obstacles because:

1. _____
   _____

2. _____

_____

3. _____

_____

affirm

I face each obstacle as an opportunity for growth and change.

When I persevere in spite of obstacles and other perils, I

_____

_____

~ week 29 ~

Unfold Your Path

I am one of those who never knows the direction of my journey until I have almost arrived.
—Anna Louise Strong, *I Changed Worlds* (1935)

ask

1. Do I ever follow someone else's path instead of my own?
2. Do I generally trust my inner compass?
3. How often do I think of my life as an unfolding journey?
4. Am I comfortable not knowing exactly where my path is leading me?
5. Am I willing to take parallel journeys—the journey that takes me out into the world and the one that pulls me within?
6. Do I focus too much on the outcomes and lose sight of the journey?
7. If I could change directions tomorrow, where would I turn?

*Y*our journey won't always reflect the seemingly clear and purposeful nature of your dreams. But that doesn't mean that you should surrender en route. First, you won't always know the length of your journey. It could last a day or a lifetime. Second, you may need to shift your point of view. If you're too focused on your destination, you will miss opportunities along the way. Third, it's possible that you will select a path that's really not yours. Paul used to work in a job that required a lot of travel and celebrity schmoozing. Friends envied Paul, but his family missed him. Eventually, despite the shock and disbelief of colleagues, he quit that job and initiated an eight-month job search. The mechanics of looking for work came fairly easily to Paul. His "soul search," however, required many turns as he responded to his unfolding path. In fact, it was that part of his quest that ultimately helped Paul turn the life he lived into the life he wanted: a more fulfilling job that challenges his mind instead of his values.

"I'm very comfortable in my own skin," he says. "Moving from being driven by external forces and expectations to being driven by knowing and leveraging your own talents is very powerful. I sleep at night without worrying about what I didn't do for somebody or how I might look in someone else's eyes. I learned that not everybody goes home at night thinking about me and what I did or didn't do for them. Also, I spend almost every night with my family at home and I soak in every moment."

experiment

Listen well. Several years ago, award-winning composer Janice Hamer turned on her radio. She listens infrequently, so it was unusual for her to hear something that would immeasurably alter her path. Dr. Gottfried Wagner, the great-grandson of composer Richard Wagner, was speaking about his family and their ties to Hitler. Jan, taken with Dr. Wagner's courage in speaking out against the anti-Semitism of his family, called the station and asked how she could contact Dr. Wagner. She wrote to him and started what has become an unlikely dialogue—East Coast Jew and exiled scion of Bayreuth, Germany. Today, they are collaborating on an opera based on a memoir (*The Lost Childhood*) by Yehuda Nir, a child Holocaust survivor, on Dr. Wagner's autobiography, and on the public dialogues between the two men. "I feel as if this work somehow already exists, like a ship that's far out at sea; and it's my job to pull it in and give it an anchor," she says. "I don't think I ever would have taken this path had I not turned on the radio that day." Whether you're listening to an interview or stumble upon a few words in the newspaper, the path before you is strewn with possibilities. That you can't determine how or when these possibilities are going to converge does not diminish their dormant power.

Connect the lines. As children, we were taught and then repeatedly encouraged to connect the dots. The instruction then became embedded in us as a metaphor for traveling on our life journeys. Unfortunately, our attention on the dots—the destinations—obscures our view of the path. We forget to pay attention to where we are in the moment. As you unfold your path, try to connect the lines and let the dots take care of themselves.

Take it with you. When Valerie DeLaCruz changed careers to become a composer and performer, she took her business acumen with her. "I applied the skills that had served me well in the design business to the music industry, making cold calls and basically worming my way into it," she says. She approached people in the recording industry with the same service-oriented philosophy that helped her succeed in her earlier life. "I kept asking myself, 'How can I make their lives easier?'" she says. "They didn't have to hold my hand because I approached everything from a business perspective." A few years ago, her second album caught the attention of the president of Relentless, a Nashville recording company that eventually signed Valerie as their debut artist.

Write out your road map. Diagram your path from start to finish. Include points along the way, like your goal, roadblocks you're likely to encounter, steps you'll take to reach your goal, a list of people who can help you get there, and how often you'll work on your goal. Don't forget to ask for directions from time to time and to refill your tank, too.

practice

In the past, I haven't always allowed my path to unfold because:

1. _____

_____

2. _____

_____

3. _____

_____

Today, my path is unfolding toward:

1. _____

_____

2. _____

_____

3. _____

_____

I'll always take these parts of me on my journeys:

1. _____

_____

2. _____

_____

3. _____

_____

affirm

I know that the knowledge I glean on one path will help me grow into whatever awaits me on the next stretch of my journey.

When I unfold my path, I

_____

_____

Cultivate a Gracious Heart

Blessed are those who can give without remem-
bering, and take without forgetting.
—Elizabeth Bibesco, *Second Encyclopedia of*
Stories, Quotations, and Anecdotes (1957),
edited by Jacob Braude

ask

1. Does it make me uncomfortable to receive an unexpected gift?
2. Do I ever dwell on what I haven't received versus what I have?
3. Do I ever give so that I can get something in return?
4. In what ways do I say, "Thank you"?
5. Do I regularly count my blessings?
6. How can I show more gratitude?
7. How can a gracious heart help me wish, dream, and do?

When you cultivate a gracious heart, your world expands. Compliment someone on the way she handled a difficult situation and watch her expression turn into complete and utter joy. Tell your child that he makes you laugh when you need it most and watch his eyes dance with pride.

The people I know who've cultivated a gracious heart have at least one common characteristic: Each expresses gratitude for her good fortune. Of course they're human and periodically express frustration over some of life's complexities. But they rarely see the world as unfair. People who express their gratitude know that they cannot accomplish everything on their own. They understand and accept the notion that it's okay to ask for help. So, instead of pushing themselves to unreasonable limits—and shortchanging their efforts in the process—they get the help they need. Sharon, a mother of two young children, is pursuing her degree in social work and stays up far past her bedtime to complete her work and prepare for the following day. Yet, she's never too tired to express gratitude for the support she receives. Janice is the mother of three, one of whom has Down's syndrome. She sees the world through a lens that accentuates what's good and right with the world. "Right after Sarah was born I felt as if all my dreams were gone. But it didn't take long for me to redefine my dreams. Most of all, I wanted Sarah to have a full life and be a contributing member of our community, one that we could be a part of as well. And that's what we worked toward. We didn't want to feel isolated and alone," says Janice. "Today I see the world differently and I wouldn't change any of it. Sarah's a part of the community and we revel in that. She's even become a rebellious adolescent and I couldn't be happier." We all have blessings to be thankful for, which makes it easy to cultivate a gracious heart.

experiment

Count your blessings. Count your blessings when you lie down at night. First, think about the blessings of the day, and then the week, until finally you're expressing thanks for the big picture. When you open your eyes in the morning, repeat the ritual, only this time consider the blessings that may occur during the day. This will put you in a gracious state of mind, which will help you attract abundance like a moth to an outdoor light.

Write them down. Write down your blessings. Whatever comes to mind. Consider your kind postal carrier who delivers a letter even when postage is due. Acknowledge the hard work of city employees who trim trees and pick up trash to make the environment more beautiful—anyone and everyone who enhances your life in big and small ways.

Keep a stash of cards and stamps. Nothing warms the heart like a handwritten note of thanks. Keep some cards and stamps handy so that you can respond quickly when someone extends a kindness. She may not even remember what she did, but she'll never forget that you took the time to express your gratitude.

Wear the lens of abundance. Focus more on gifts you've received and less on what you think you deserve. Assuming that mind-set will ease your stress and help you turn away from the tendency to compare yourself to others. We heard this when we were young and it's still true today: Sometimes you'll have more than others; sometimes you'll have less. But if you're constantly trying to measure up to what others have, you will never recognize or appreciate what securely resides in your heart.

practice

It's not easy for me to cultivate a gracious heart when:

1. _____

_____

2. _____

_____

3. _____

_____

I have always shown my gratitude when:

1. _____

_____

2. _____

_____

3. _____

_____

I can cultivate a gracious heart by:

1. _____

_____

2. _____

_____

3. _____

_____

affirm

I think less about what I want and more about my current and past good fortune.

When I cultivate a gracious heart, I

_____

_____

Go to a Room of Your Own

*I have at last got the little room I have wanted
so long, and am very happy about it. It does me
good to be alone.*
—Louisa May Alcott, *Journals* (1868)

ask

1. What do I have in common with others (such as artists, writers, sculptors, dancers, and accountants) who've benefited from having a room of their own?
2. What would I put into a room of my own?
3. What can I remember about some of my favorite rooms?
4. Who might lend me a room of my own? Could I reciprocate?
5. Do I need to put aside some money to help me secure a room of my own?
6. Must a room of my own have four walls and a door?
7. Would a room of my own help me turn what I want into what is mine?

Do you long for a space to call your own? If you're very lucky, you might have a room of your own. Even a corner or a closet will do when you absolutely, positively need to be alone. Whether you're writing fiction, reading an important letter, or praying for a miracle, the work you do toward achieving your dreams deserves a separate space.

Remember, too, that a room of your own won't necessarily have four walls. Your room might be a park vista seen from a favorite bench. Or your room might stretch across a few feet of the shoreline of a lake, river, or ocean. Perhaps you'll find a room within a room. I've been known to hide out in my closet. I did it as a kid and I do it today. By definition, a room of your own will be what and where you need it to be.

When author Victoria Moran is in the middle of writing a book, she camps out at a certain coffee establishment at the corner of eighty-sixth and Columbus in New York City. For her, the large table that seats about eight signifies a time and place that suggests uninterrupted work and creativity. "I know exactly what I'm going to do at that table," she says. "It's a specific place where my body and mind come together so that I can focus." Like Victoria, you can learn how to enter a space that becomes your inner kingdom, a remarkable and unique retreat that is yours alone. Indeed, this has been the setting for the creation of nine of Victoria's published books.

experiment

Borrow a room. As I worked on my last book occasionally I would slip into the calm and quiet home of my friend Judith. She had graciously offered her space as an alternative for me during busy weekends when I felt torn between family and work. I would sit at the dining room table surrounded by cream-colored walls and a sense of order that is sometimes in short supply at my address. My inspiration often took the form of ice cream that beckoned from Judith's freezer. Think of people you know who might be willing to lend you a room. Reciprocate whenever possible. And replace that pint of ice cream if necessary.

Revisit an old room. Take on the role of a home inspector, walk around with a clipboard and pen, and make note of spots that could be transformed into an area that could become—even temporarily—your room. For instance, if a chair normally reserved for guests suddenly becomes your comfort zone, well, your visitors might just have to share their sitting rights.

Claim a public room. Look around your community and you're likely to discover rooms that are accessible, welcoming, and inspiring at the same time. As a reader, you may revel within the quiet rooms in a public library. Perhaps you can find a gallery where the works of art bring out the artist in you. Even an outdoor room in a park or garden can offer a peaceful respite from the distractions that keep you from reaching your potential. If you find yourself saying, "I wish I could do this more often," after you leave your new room, find a way to fulfill this modest desire. Just because your name isn't attached to a particular address doesn't mean you don't belong there.

practice

Rooms I have visited:

1. _____

_____

2. _____

_____

3. _____

_____

When I walked into these rooms, I felt:

1. _____
   _____

2. _____
   _____

3. _____
   _____

My favorite room brings out the best in me because:

1. _____
   _____

2. _____
   _____

3. _____
   _____

affirm

When I go to a room of my own I leave behind the static that prevents me from clearly visualizing my dreams.

When I go to a room of my own, I

_____

_____

Carry a Three-Way Mirror

It is a fault to wish to be understood before we
have made ourselves clear to ourselves.
—Simone Weil, *Gravity and Grace* (1947)

ask

1. Am I surprised when someone notices something I've said or done?
2. Am I willing to see what others see in me? The good and the not so good?
3. Do I regularly stand back and "watch" myself from the outside looking in?
4. Am I afraid of what I might see?
5. If I see something I don't like, am I willing to change?
6. Are there days when I don't care who I am or what I see?
7. Do I understand the connection between knowing myself and pursuing my dreams?

I have never liked three-way mirrors, especially the ones illuminated by fluorescent lights. Still, I am always a little intrigued by the perspectives offered in each reflection. I like to imagine that one mirror reflects who we are, the second whom we'd like to be, and the third how others see us. Sometimes as you wish, dream, and do you will wonder who you are and how you got to where you're standing today. You'll also think about how the people in your life—past, present, and future—influence your desire to turn the life you're living into the life you want. Don't let other people's influence diminish who you are. We're all somebody's someone—a daughter, a partner, a sister. But we will always be our own selves. And the more you know about yourself—and are willing to admit—the better off you'll be as you embark on a journey that's authentic and fulfilling. For example, if you need external reinforcement as you near the completion of a major project, ask your loved ones to cheer you on. If a stark office leaves your imagination cool and unreceptive, add personal items like family pictures and inspirational quotes to your work space. If morning is the only time you can fit in exercise, plan your day accordingly so that you're not distracted by what you wish you'd done six hours earlier.

On some days we know exactly who we are and what we want. Like a set of essential reference texts, our self-knowledge is bulging with facts, figures, and illustrations—we know what we look like, our goals are precise, and there's no question that we're doing exactly what we were meant to do. But life rarely progresses so smoothly. Interruptions throw our equilibrium out of whack, and just as we think we've got it all together we're asking ourselves, "How did that just happen? How did I get *here*?" Carrying a three-way mirror—and taking it out, too—is one way to clarify and understand your purpose. You may not always like what you see, but you will learn about the person you really are, and that alone will enhance your journey. Ask yourself, for example, if, amid your job search, you've paid enough attention to your personal life. If you have children, are they getting the best of you or a slice of your worn-out self? Do you share your frustrations with your partner or do you keep them bottled up inside? Is there a relationship you'd like to fix or end altogether?

When we don't take the time to know ourselves—our strengths, weaknesses, likes, and dislikes—we shortchange our ability to make a contribution to the world and to our lives. If you don't know who you are now, how can you possibly turn into the person you'd like to be?

experiment

Be open to the mirror, mirror on the wall. Look at your eyes. Do they express your dreams? What about your smile? Is it sincere or are you hiding a certain sorrow? Sometimes we just need to look in the mirror and reassure ourselves that we're here with something important to do. Say it out loud to your reflection. You might be surprised by what you hear.

Identify and validate from within. Hearing what people say is one thing. Allowing their words to tell us what we can be is quite another. In spite of our big ideas—starting a new business, changing careers, having a baby after age forty—other people can make us feel small. If you're going to turn the life you're living into the life you want, you must reject the idea of letting other people define who you are.

Clean your mirror. Sometimes our lives are obscured by situations and circumstances that settle over us like a stubborn layer of dust. But all it takes is one big sweeping motion to clear things off and start again. It's possible, for instance, to recognize once and for all that finance just isn't your thing. Maybe you've excelled at numbers and fulfilled a parent's dream to follow in his shoes, yet you know in your heart that you'd be happier helping people by becoming a health-care worker. Instead of accepting the status quo, sign up for a workshop that will introduce you to the field. Remember that no one ever put a limit on the number of times that you can start over.

practice

In the past, accepting my shortcomings felt:

1. _____

_____

2. _____

_____

3. _____

_____

I can work toward seeing the person I am and the person I want to be by doing the following:

1. _____

_____

2. _____

_____

3. _____

_____

Knowing who I am isn't about fear; it's about:

1. _____

_____

2. _____

_____

3. _____

_____

affirm

The way I'm perceived by others can never alter who I am and what I stand for.

When I carry my three-way mirror, I

_____

_____

Stay in School

*It made me gladsome to be getting some edu-
cation, it being like a big window opening.*
—Mary Webb, *Precious Bane* (1924)

ask

1. Do I learn something new every day?
2. In what three areas would I like to expand my knowledge?
3. As a child, did I enjoy school?
4. What is my favorite school memory?
5. Do I still have teachers who make a difference in my life?
6. What would I study if I were to go back to school?
7. Are my mistakes an opportunity to learn?

If you're like most people, you couldn't wait to get out of school and into the "real" world where you could be your own boss, use four-letter words with impunity, and stay up past midnight. Yet, even the real world can make you restless, especially when your mind and body ache for spring breaks and summer vacations. We can't go back in time, but we can immerse ourselves in environments that stimulate our intellects.

Staying in school isn't about becoming a professional student. Rather, it's about expanding your knowledge both horizontally and vertically. You may finish a course or complete a degree, but you're never finished with learning. You're never going to know everything, so why not be open to broadening your base? If we wish and dream with a finite set of assets, we limit our potential by basing what we know on a mere snapshot versus an ever-evolving image. What might have been fresh two weeks ago could be stale within a month. This is especially true in the business world where technology and economics converge daily to effect change in every sector.

Staying in school is, at the very least, an attitude. It's accepting the notion that each day you can soak up new experiences that can enhance your journey. But it's more than merely accumulating an encyclopedic sort of knowledge. If you're simply picking up facts and statistics without mulling them over and discovering where they fit into your life, you're not going to get closer to your goal. For example, if you read the technology section of the newspaper, think about how a new technology will affect industries that you work with or want to work with. Or, instead of waiting until you've completed an eight-week workshop, take the knowledge you get on the first night back to your office and apply it the next day.

It doesn't take much, though, to stay in school every single day. I'm not suggesting that you never skip class, but while you're playing hooky—whether you're at the movies or driving downtown for a day in the city—take it all in from a student's point of view. You won't be tested, at least in the conventional sense, so relax and enjoy.

experiment

Stay in school online. Sign up for an online course. The areas from which to choose are infinite. Do your homework, though, before you make a commitment and make sure the sponsoring organization is legitimate, especially if there is a fee. Or, log on to www.npr.org and watch and listen as your world expands. Listening to public radio is a little like auditing your favorite class. You come and go as you please and with little exception you're likely to discover something you didn't know before.

Sign up for a class or workshop. Sign up for a course at your local public library, YMCA, or any number of organizations in your community. Bring plenty of business cards if you have them. Class breaks and the times before and after are great opportunities for connecting with others.

Create a library. You don't need much to create a library under your own roof. All it requires is a shelf or some baskets (or both) where you can stash your collection. Start small and purchase books that fall within your budget. The idea is to have ready access to the areas of interest that are closest to your dreams. Stock up on writing guides if you want to write a novel. Purchase a few interior design books if you'd like to become a decorator. Magazines, too, are a wonderful and rich resource. Subscribe to one or two. Also, let your circle of support (friends, family, and mentors) know that you're building a home library and would be grateful for any materials they want to donate.

practice

Learning is an ongoing process for me because:

1. _____

_____

2. _____

_____

3. _____

_____

I've always wanted to know more about:

1. _____

_____

2. _____

_____

3. _____

_____

I can "stay in school" by adding the following activities to my life:

1. _____

_____

2. _____

_____

3. _____

_____

affirm

For as long as we're living we can make discoveries about the world and about ourselves.

When I "stay in school," I

_____

_____

Wait with Charm and Patience

Everyone has their time and kind of waiting.
—Elizabeth Gaskell, *Mary Barton* (1848)

ask

1. Am I a patient person?
2. How do I usually handle situations that require patience?
3. Am I willing to practice being patient in spite of my natural tendencies to act otherwise?
4. Whom do I admire for her patience? What can I learn from her?
5. How could I benefit by being more patient?
6. Can I be patient but effectively plan for the future as well?
7. How could my life be better if I were more patient?

In these do-it-now-or-never times, patience doesn't seem like such a virtue. If you don't do something fast enough, someone else might do it first. If success doesn't happen overnight, well, perhaps you're not as good as you thought you were. Still, immediate success cannot compare to the exhilarating experience of watching something unfold over time. Think of the thrilling moment when a baby finally takes her first steps after a series of false starts and stumbles. Then, replay your moments of measured success—a longstanding project finally coming to fruition, making amends after an extended period of conflict, or finishing a degree after years of study (and maybe with a full-time job and a family to juggle).

A few years ago my mother and I talked about her struggle to obtain first a college degree and then a master's in counseling. In her fifties, working full-time, it took her twelve long years to achieve her dream. "How could you wait so long?" I asked her. "I never expected to graduate," she said. Early in my mother's life she'd been discouraged from going to school. Instead, she was told to go to work so that she could contribute to the household income. When she finally was able to go back to school she embraced each class for the pure joy of learning that had been denied so many years earlier.

Pursuing your passion really occurs on parallel paths: One path highlights the destination, the other focuses on the journey. Neither path is better than the other, nor can one exist without the other.

Sometimes we short-change the benefits of being patient. The word is so firmly associated with virtue that we forget the tangible results that patience can bring. Patience can help you become a better listener. For example, if you have a tendency to interrupt people when they're speaking, consciously practicing patience will help you break that habit or at least minimize it. You'll absorb more information. Indeed, people will be drawn to you because of your good listening skills. Plus, you'll be less likely to miss things (like people's first names when being introduced). Patient listening often yields grand results like more self-discipline and compassion for others. You'll also achieve a sense of calm that will be useful as you work hard to achieve your dreams.

experiment

Recall triumphs in your past. Sometimes when we're waiting anxiously for good things to happen we forget about our past successes, times when our hard work and patience paid off. Things get really out of control when our inability to wait coincides with our lack of confidence—in ourselves and in the future. Dissolve that toxic mix by recalling a time when you successfully allowed time to move by itself, without your intervention. Play that role again whenever necessary.

Get inspired. Often we marvel at other people's successes, focusing solely on the results—more money, bigger house, notoriety. Yet, how often do we imagine the hardships endured along the way? Was the path a grueling one? What kinds of sacrifices were made? Did she ever want to give up? Did she get enough support? Even if we cannot answer those questions, it's useful to ask them anyway and try, for a moment, to imagine how a person has gotten from one point to another. That's when we realize that even a reported "overnight success" is anything but.

Wait your turn. When Dave Thomas, the founder of Wendy's Old Fashioned Hamburgers, died, a slew of articles popped up, most of them highlighting the visionary's single-mindedness and patience. Waiting your turn isn't just about being polite. It's about knowing when the time is right—recognizing when others will be receptive to a particular idea, whether it's square-shaped fast food or rings that change colors according to your mood. Dave Thomas did this with burgers and made history.

Be patient with yourself. Whether you run your own show or report to a boss, doling out some patience for yourself is essential if you want to succeed. Sometimes you will be your own greatest challenge. You'll get in your own way, trip all over yourself, and then step into dangerous territory—self-doubt. Jerry Cleaver, founder and creator of The Writer's Loft in Chicago, says that the biggest problem threatening our creativity is ourselves. "Your emotions are your best guide, your trusted friend really," he says. "Yet, when your emotions begin telling you that your ideas aren't good or that you're wasting your time, you stop working and your creativity is thwarted. How can you possibly defend yourself?"

practice

Sometimes I become impatient with others when:

1. _____

_____

2. _____

_____

3. _____

_____

I get impatient with myself when:

1. _____

_____

2. _____

_____

3. _____

_____

In the past, I've been patient when:

1. _____

_____

2. _____

_____

3. _____

_____

affirm

When I am patient, long lines are shorter, I get what I need more quickly, and I am exactly where I need to be.

When I wait with charm and grace, I

_____

_____

Find Grace in the Balance

Grace fills empty spaces, but it can only enter where there is a void to receive it, and it is grace itself which makes this void.
—Simone Weil, *Gravity and Grace* (1947)

ask

1. How easily do I accept what I can't always explain?
2. How do I define *grace*?
3. Does this higher power believe in me no matter what?
4. Can I articulate my beliefs in a greater power?
5. Do I still believe that if I do something wrong, "God will punish me"?
6. Is God—or some kind of higher power—in a part of me?
7. What, if any, are my expectations of including grace in my life?

Many years ago, during a Sunday-school lesson, the teacher said, "There's a part of God in all of you." Her words made a huge and indelible impression on me. I remember thinking, Wow! God could be in my arms or my legs or my toes! Clearly, I was amazed by this, and to this day I am convinced that, even on my worst hair days, there is a part of God in me.

When we recognize something greater than ourselves, the world with all its upside-down craziness seems a little more serene, not so frantic. Think of a dimmer switch that helps soften a room. Like the switch that creates a sense of calm, finding grace in the balance minimizes the glare of a fast-paced, out-of-control life.

Inviting grace into your journey ensures the presence of a steady, spiritual companion—a quiet yet powerful force that will keep you tethered to your path. Marilyn, a journalist, says that the religious precepts taught to her as a child give her comfort. "The principles that guide me also help me define my priorities," says Marilyn. "If a friend or relative needs help, for instance, it feels quite natural for me to tend to that person's needs if at all possible. I enjoy my work, but it's the combination of that and my beliefs that makes me happy. The joy I've experienced comes largely from the satisfaction of honoring the divine presence in my life. I can't obtain real satisfaction if I feel I've cheated what I believe is really the right thing to do."

Whether you call it a higher self, a greater power, God, or nothing at all, maintaining some sense of the divine will fill you with hope and compassion. This is essential as you make your way on the wish it, dream it, do it journey. Think of grace as a signpost that's always a step ahead of your efforts, offering a constant message that says "you can do this." Without grace, you may feel alone and subsequently unable to manage the hard work of your dreams.

When you look for and find grace in the balance, you make contact with an old but sturdy lighthouse—the one within your soul that illuminates all your journeys. Like the lighthouse that guides the sailor with an intermittent beam of light, grace is a beacon of hope and strength.

experiment

Find it where you can. Find it in the shower at night, where your only job is to stand under a stream of hot water, or waiting in the carpool line, or even standing in the checkout at the grocery store. Find grace wherever you can. It parks nowhere in particular but gets around just the same.

Accept what you can't always explain. Get comfortable with miracles and the less-than-stellar moments, too. Accept the ups, the downs, and everything in between. Whether you're amazed at your good luck or devastated by a new disappointment, a little grace goes a long way. It will quiet that pesky voice that keeps asking for a neat and convenient resolution.

Observe grace in others. Author Victoria Moran is a master at finding grace in the balance. She brings a perspective to her life, and the lives of her readers, that illuminates all possibilities. Like the title of one of her books, Victoria is "lit from within." She exudes a sense of gratitude and a quiet hopefulness in the world around her. In her presence, people feel good about themselves because she shows them, through her books and in workshops, how anyone can create a radiance that comes from within. She is not afraid to wish, dream, and do, and even amid uncertainty Victoria presses on in her efforts to turn the life she's living into the life she wants.

practice

I have difficulty finding grace in the balance when:

1. _____

_____

2. _____

_____

3. _____

_____

Sometimes I see glimmers of grace that look like:

1. _____

_____

2. _____

_____

3. _____

_____

I'm open to a spiritual practice that will enable me to:

1. _____

_____

2. _____

_____

3. _____

_____

affirm

With grace by my side I am always able to find my way home.

When I find grace in the balance, I

_____

_____

~ week 36 ~

Apprehend Your
Mood Thieves

*I was so mad you could have boiled a pot of
water on my head.*
—Alice Childress, *Creative Experience* (1924)

ask

1. Am I getting enough sleep?
2. Am I eating mostly healthful foods?
3. Am I getting enough exercise?
4. Do I seem overly sensitive?
5. Do I regularly snap at friends and family?
6. Do rainy, overcast days get me down?
7. Has anything changed in my life recently?

"She's in a bad mood." I've always hated when people say that, especially when I'm the "she." Not only have I been found out but labeled so that no one wants anything to do with me. "She's in a bad mood" might also mean: "She had a fight with her husband/partner/lover"; "She got her period"; or "She had a bad day at work." Besides feeling crummy, we can incur some serious damage around us. Our work suffers, too.

Apprehending your mood thieves takes careful planning and

some practice. At first, you may consider the solutions unproven or simply too difficult to master. But it's not that hard; it takes only a few changes. More rest, a nutritious diet, and regular exercise can significantly alter and improve your moods.

Over the last few years the study of moods has taken on a more serious tone. That's the good news. The not-so-good news is that we're still underestimating how effectively we can help ourselves face the blues. In many cases, we don't need a pill or a fad diet. We just need a change in attitude, one that will last. Sometimes we shift outlooks after experiencing a health scare, either our own or a loved one's. You may read the results of a major study and conclude for yourself that a change is necessary. Or a friend might introduce you to a new form of exercise that becomes a regular part of your life. Let's face it: When you're in a bad mood or are feeling cranky, you're not likely to make a good impression—on a boss, a child, a spouse, or anyone else who's important in your life. Instead of letting your bad mood influence your actions, grab hold of it and salvage what you can before it causes irreparable damage.

experiment

Edit your speech. Refrain from saying "I'm in a bad mood" each time you feel out of sorts. Instead, figure out where the mood thief is coming from. Are you disappointed? Did someone annoy you before your day even began? Are you feeling overwhelmed? Replace bad-mood language with a new script like, "Here they come again. I think I'll head them off by . . ." (taking a walk, eating a healthy lunch, calling an old friend, smiling on a fond memory).

Move your bones. Jump, stretch, walk, run, swim, and climb. Exercising helps bring oxygen to your body's cells and can assist in regulating brain chemicals. It's also good for your metabolism. You'll soon see that endorphins—those substances we produce all by ourselves during exercise—really can bring on a natural high.

Drink up. In addition to flushing out physical toxins, water can miraculously rid your body of a sour disposition. Drink at least eight glasses a day and you're likely to cut down on the other stuff—coffee, soda (packed with caffeine, sugar, or artificial sweeteners), and alcohol—which can actually invite the mood thieves in for a not-so-nice visit.

Heal with light and color. For thousands of years people all over the world have applied light and color in the practice of medicine. Some colors, like blues and greens, can actually create a tranquil effect, which can help dissipate a bad mood. If you're light deprived, it might show up in sluggish movement or a decrease in your energy level. So, open the blinds, sit by a window when you can, dress up in your happiest shade of anything, and keep a 64-count box of Crayola crayons nearby.

Get help. Don't be afraid to seek professional help if you're unable to shake free of mood swings and anxiety. A good therapist and/or physician familiar with mood disorders will help you return to a healthy equilibrium so that you can get back to turning the life you're living into the life you want.

practice

I consistently get into a bad mood when:

1. _____

_____

2. _____

_____

3. _____

_____

If I can more effectively manage my moods, the people whom I love will:

1. _____

_____

2. _____

_____

3. _____

_____

This week I will commit to changing the way I respond to my moods by:

1. _____

_____

2. _____

_____

3. _____

_____

affirm

When I apprehend my mood thieves, I am less anxious, experience fewer angry episodes, and am better equipped to handle stress.

When I apprehend my mood thieves, I

_____

_____

~ week 37 ~

Protect and Nourish Your Soul

We make ourselves our own distress,
We are ourselves our happiness.
—L. E. Landon, title poem,
The Troubadour (1825)

ask

1. Do I agree to do things for others and later regret those decisions?
2. Do I sometimes forget that it's okay for me to stand up for myself?
3. Are my boundaries ever invaded? By whom? When? Why?
4. Do I ever wait for others to set my boundaries?
5. Am I aware of and do I have respect for other people's boundaries?
6. Is it hard for me to put my own needs first? Do I equate self-care with being selfish?
7. Do I ever lose touch with my real self, the self that gives me power over my life?

People cross boundaries all the time, yet we minimize the intrusion or repress it. Often the way we respond is tied up with how we feel about ourselves—our self-value, our worth. Maybe a friend comments on the way your fourteen-year-old daughter dresses for school. Perhaps a coworker shares confidential information about you with your supervisor. A relative may ask how you paid for a luxury item on your salary. You can ignore the comment, but the absence of a response can erode your boundaries as well.

To stave off boundary invasions, you must commit to do the following: (1) accept the notion that having boundaries is your birthright; (2) determine your boundaries; and (3) enforce your boundaries without guilt. If you can't draw boundaries you remain a moving target; people—friends, family, coworkers, and strangers— will not respect or recognize where they end and you begin.

Boundaries help us determine which behaviors are acceptable and which behaviors are not—for others and for ourselves. A strong boundary shines a spotlight on your needs and, like a warm and comforting blanket, securely encircles your mind, body, and spirit.

When we neglect our boundaries and allow them to be violated, we move further from our dreams. We begin to let others dictate our success. Our voices become quieter and quieter until all we hear are the needs and unsolicited opinions of others. For example, if someone with whom you've shared a dream begins to openly analyze your plan and motives or speculates on the improbability of your wishes, she's crossed a boundary. Protect yourself first by letting her know that you're unhappy with her remarks and then explain succinctly and firmly that you will no longer talk with her about your dreams. If you respect your boundaries and treat them with compassion and care, they become your safe haven, even if only in your mind. Of course, it's not always easy to set and strengthen boundaries. If you're accustomed to pleasing others at the cost of your own well-being, for example, setting boundaries may feel awkward. Yet, before you can expect to benefit from boundaries you must become acutely self-aware—know your likes and dislikes, strengths and weaknesses, your history, hopes, and roles (partner, sibling, child, colleague, etc.), and how you'd like to be remembered.

experiment

Set and maintain limits. Naturally, this is probably the hardest but most important step to take when establishing boundaries. Make a list of what you will not tolerate in others. For example, write, "I will not allow others to shout at me, borrow my personal belongings without asking, or humiliate me in front of my peers." Return to this list as often as necessary and ask yourself how effective you are at maintaining the limits. Later, add a list of your personal "rights," reasonable expectations that will keep you intact emotionally, physically, and spiritually—direct answers from your doctor, a few minutes of peace each night after the kids have gone to bed, everyone pitching in to help around the house, and so on.

Speak up. Sometimes we get tongue-tied not because we have so much to say but because we don't know how to say it. It is critical that you speak up—whether you're asking for what you need or expressing your disapproval of the way you've been treated. It's amazing how others will respond to your language when you speak up with confidence, kindness, and resolve. Don't expect people to give you permission to speak up; it is your birthright and your responsibility to ask for what you need. Use language that imparts understanding and respect: "Next time we review my work, could you please talk to me without raising your voice?"; "It makes me feel small and bad when you speak to me in that tone"; "Could we talk in private the next time we disagree about the kids?"

Observe successful boundary keepers. Occasionally, nothing brings clarity to the surface more quickly than watching others. If a peer consistently and successfully sets boundaries, observe her methods. Ask her how she succeeds. You might say, "I've noticed that you're very good at protecting your business interests. Can you give me some tips you've used in the past?" This is especially important if you're creating a new product or slogan. If you say "yes" when you really mean "no," think of a friend or colleague who isn't afflicted with the same need to please. Ask her how she does it. Take notes if necessary. And then start practicing. Don't answer the phone if you're busy. Inform your teenage children that you're not to be disturbed. Reschedule an appointment if you're not feeling well.

Look back. If you grew up in a family that did not define and respect boundaries, you might have trouble doing so as an adult. But your history is no excuse for letting those boundaries go. One of the best places to start is with your relationships, which are defined by boundaries. If your privacy was violated as a child, you may be particularly sensitive when someone probes and tries to elicit more information from you than you're willing to share. If someone else's happiness was dependent on your behavior, you may have difficulty accepting the notion that you bring joy to other people's lives.

practice

I need to have boundaries because:

1. _____

_____

2. _____

_____

3. _____

_____

I am uncomfortable when people:

1. _____

_____

2. _____

_____

3. _____

_____

It is okay for me to expect:

1. _____

_____

2. _____

_____

3. _____

_____

affirm

When I protect and nourish my soul, I show others how to do the same for themselves.

When I protect and nourish my soul, I

_____

_____

~ week 38 ~

Choose Process over Outcome

The events in our lives happen in a sequence in time, but in their significance to ourselves, they find their own order . . . the continuous thread of revelation.

—Eudora Welty, *One Writer's Beginnings* (1984)

ask

1. If I had the choice, would I rather know what's next and be prepared or accept whatever happens and mostly be surprised?
2. Do I tend to neglect the process in favor of the outcome?
3. Can the process really be as sweet as the success?
4. Does the process ever slow me down? Is that necessarily a bad thing?
5. Can I learn how to embrace the process when I've focused for so long on the outcome, the mission?
6. Am I comfortable and satisfied with the ebb and flow of my life?
7. What am I doing today to enhance the flow of my life?

It's not easy to live our lives in process. Our culture is so focused on outcomes, products, and solutions that we downgrade and diminish how we get from one day to the next. With our senses fixed on what's *going* to happen, we give short shrift to our awareness of the here and now. Keeping your eye on the prize is fine. But what if the prize is moving along right beside you? Your efforts to wish, dream, and do could be divided into two columns—process and outcome. Yet, without your mindful participation, your accomplishments will be hollow, missing the substance and grist of life that characterizes an evolving journey.

Choosing process over outcome makes sense as more and more people, particularly women, struggle with work/life integration issues. Several years ago, equipped with an MBA from Northwestern University, Kathy McDonald got promoted from one marketing job to another. However, she had little time to savor her accomplishments. Though successful in business, Kathy's personal life suffered. "We live in an 'accomplishment' culture," she says. "When you're on a track to move from one success to another, the satisfaction you derive becomes fleeting. There's just not enough time to enjoy it. For me, leaving the corporate world was okay. Some people absolutely need to know how their career paths are going to unfold. People who go out on their own need, to some extent, to be comfortable with not knowing what's next. In that case, the process becomes the focus."

Today, Kathy is a mother and a successful freelance writer, consultant, and coauthor of *Creating Your Life Collage: Strategies for Solving the Work/Life Dilemma,* a book she was inspired to write after recognizing her work/life dilemma. These days, it is Kathy's awareness of process that helps her maintain and live within a flow of life that is consistent with her needs and values. "For the most part, I trust my life is unfolding as it should at a pace that I can live with," she says.

experiment

Compare with compassion. It's natural to compare your life process with someone else's. It's normal, too, to compare your progression with the ideal—how you might have imagined your life to be. Don't get stuck on comparisons, though. Pluck out the useful bits and then move on. For example, if you haven't been able to replicate the perfect job you had out of college, think about what you liked so much and attempt to find it in your next position. If a friend experiences a spiritual awakening, ask her how it happened and then apply the knowledge to your own life. Try not to mourn what hasn't happened and instead prepare yourself for the wonderful, unexplored possibilities.

Ask who, what, where, and how every day. Ask yourself each day where you are on your life's continuum. Are you where you want to be? Are you on course? Have you forgotten an important piece? Can you delay something due to unforeseen circumstances? For that moment, find out who you are, what you're doing, and where and how you're doing it. If the exercise becomes tiresome, cut it back to once a week, preferably at around the same time. Put a Post-it on your bathroom mirror or on your night table as a reminder. Try to refrain from judging your answers. You're just collecting bits and pieces that make up the journey.

Use process as a verb. Unlike outcomes and solutions, process puts you into action. It means you're moving, changing, and adapting, which are requirements for wishing, dreaming, and doing. Use this principle as you move along the wish-it path. When you feel stuck, for instance, remind yourself that you're processing your life, mixing and combining a variety of ingredients. We process our dreams, our experiences, and even our fears so that we understand more fully why we're here and what we're meant to do.

practice

In the past, my process has been interrupted by:

1. _____

_____

2. _____

_____

3. _____

_____

I can reconcile process and outcome by:

1. _____

_____

2. _____

_____

3. _____

_____

I can begin to view my life as a process by:

1. _____

_____

2. _____

_____

3. _____

_____

affirm

By living in process, I continually discover things about myself that I didn't know before.

When I choose process over outcome, I

_____

_____

~ week 39 ~

Listen to Your Quiet

Silence was the first prayer I learned to trust.
—Patricia Hampl, *Virgin Time* (1992)

ask

1. Do I consider my voice important?
2. Do I ever push my inner voice aside, afraid of what I might hear?
3. Do I equate not talking with having nothing to say?
4. Can I listen to my quiet without judging?
5. Do I seek out opportunities to listen to my quiet?
6. Am I open to new ways of listening to my quiet?
7. Do I give myself at least five to ten minutes a day to hear my thoughts?

Do you ever listen to your quiet—those unexpected, dropped-right-from-the-sky moments when your own thoughts can actually be heard over the din encircling your life? Sometimes we're afraid to listen to our own voices or the silence in the night or the drone of a distant plane. You may feel as if the quiet is an uncomfortable void—a dreaded emptiness—instead of a beautiful and treasured gift. For years, I used to fill my quiet with other voices. Whom can I call while I prepare dinner? What show can I watch? What do I do with all this *quiet?*

Instead of embracing our quiet, we push it away or we constantly try to fill it up. It's like having a surface that's never clear. Yet, in order to follow your dreams, you must create an environment—a platform, really—in which your dreams can speak. Without such a platform your dreams remain shapeless and stuck between potential and movement. To give your dreams a voice, you must think about what you want to accomplish. In other words, ask yourself each day, "What is today's mission and how can I get there?" It is within this quiet space that your dreams can be heard. Listening in this way reinforces where you want to be. It also forces you to confront problems and face self-doubt head-on. Sometimes our dreams speak quietly. After all, we may not want anyone to hear. But if *you're* not listening, well, you've gone too far. Don't confuse listening to your quiet with silencing your voice. Indeed, listening to your quiet is essential if you are to hear the conversation deep within your heart and soul—an acceptable and highly fashionable form of eavesdropping.

A common reason (or is it an excuse?) for not listening to our quiet is our habit of listening to and surrounding ourselves by others. But solitude—a necessary state of mind for hearing your inner voice—doesn't necessarily mean the absence of others. Listening to your voice, even those inconsequential, uneven stream-of-consciousness bursts of discovery, is the very best way to *be present with yourself.* If you are exclusively aware of others, your self will be harder and harder to distinguish and your quiet will be less than a whisper.

As you learn to listen to your quiet, it will become second nature. You might not even be aware of what you're doing. That, of course, is the idea. You might discover that your quiet isn't so void of noise after all. Alison, a marketing vice president for a publishing company, simply closes her door and instructs her assistant to take all her calls. "I know that unless I take that time to really focus, I'm never going to reach the answer I'm looking for," she says. "Naturally, others things have to wait and certainly I might have a stack of messages that need attention once I open the door. But that's okay because once I've had time to just think about the problem, the solution is much more apparent to me."

experiment

Go on a silent retreat. Chris visits a monastery every six months, where she simply listens to what's going on around and within. For two and a half days, she doesn't speak. Often, her listening turns to gratitude. She's grateful, she says, to God for not giving her what she wants. Not surprisingly, she discovers on this quiet journey that what she couldn't hear before becomes loud and clear and often *different* from what she envisioned for her life—what she originally wanted or thought she wanted. If you can't get away for a silent retreat, create one at home or in your car or standing in line waiting for the train. Avoid seeking the ideal situation as the ideal is often unobtainable. Do the next best thing.

Save your quiet. More than likely, your days preclude the chance to listen to your quiet. "I haven't stopped for a second," you may say as you're brushing your teeth at the stroke of midnight or tucking in a child a few minutes after nine. The other night, as I sat quietly in the family room, my husband asked if I was coming upstairs. "In a minute," I said. It had been a day of carpools, fast food, and a book-group meeting in my living room. I'd enjoyed the day but needed just five or ten minutes to simply listen to what was being said inside. I had saved my quiet for the end of the day.

Pay attention to your dreams. Here, I'm referring to your sleeping dreams, the ones that have you flying, winning the lottery, or missing an entire semester of your senior year of high school. Dreams are really suppressed thoughts that we may not hear during the course of our daily lives. If something is thwarting your ability to wish, dream, and do, you might discover the source of the problem in your sleep. Don't be afraid to analyze your dreams and connect them in some way to what's going on in your wakeful life. Jot your dreams down, too; perhaps you'll discover a pattern. Our dreams can be teachers that show us how to understand and more fully believe in ourselves.

practice

Places where I can listen to my quiet:

1. _____

_____

2. _____

_____

3. _____

_____

When I listened to my quiet, this is what I heard:

1. _____

_____

2. _____

_____

3. _____

_____

When I listened to my quiet, this is how I felt:

1. _____

_____

2. _____

_____

3. _____

_____

affirm

Listening to my quiet is as valuable as reading a good book, giving to my favorite charity, or hugging someone I love.

When I listen to my quiet, I

_____

_____

Replenish Your Fun Jar

People need joy quite as much as clothing.
Some of them need it far more.
—Margaret Collier Graham,
Gifts and Givers (1906)

ask

1. When do I have the most fun?
2. As a child, what brought me unbridled joy?
3. How important is it for me to have fun?
4. How do I bring joy and fun into other people's lives?
5. Where does my joy intersect with my dreams?
6. Am I willing to examine my sorrows in order to unearth my joys?
7. Is there really a connection between having fun and being successful?

When was the last time you laughed till your belly hurt? When was the last time you smiled at a fond memory? Like a neglected cookie jar that contains only crumbs, we forget to replenish ourselves with fun and joy. We even get used to that empty feeling, as if filling it would upset our steady and familiar equilibrium.

Sometimes a rut robs us of our joy. Perhaps we don't see progress fast enough or we sabotage our joy and instead of moving forward we dwell on our bad luck. So how do you get it back?

Begin with openness toward the unexpected. Consider joy for what it is, not for what it may or may not lead to. Joy in and of itself isn't success, financial security, fame, or respect. Those are things that can make life easier but they're not what truly make us happy.

Joyfulness is almost indescribable, yet it wields tremendous power and influence. If you really intend to integrate the life you're living into the life you want, you must replenish the part of your spirit that absolutely, positively lifts you high above the stress and struggle that's part of your day. Danielle, a small-business owner, isn't fond of bookkeeping though she knows that for her company to thrive she needs to tend to the numbers. "On the days when I'm steeped in numbers I tend to leave that stuff in the office when I go home. Once I'm there, I'll play superheroes with my son. He's Superman and I'm Wonderwoman. I tie his blanket around his shoulders and then he goes flying around the house," says Danielle. "For the moment, bookkeeping doesn't matter anymore."

experiment

Go back. Remember something from your childhood that brought you pure, unencumbered joy. Think about how you can bring that old fun back to life. You may not have access to the same tree house, but maybe you can evoke a similar feeling by creating a private nook in your home. Perhaps it's an old-fashioned tea party that will help replenish your fun jar. It doesn't matter what you come up with; allowing yourself the pleasure is what really counts.

Try something once. You don't have to be a thrill seeker to imagine what you might do once in your life. Even the imagining is enough to put you in a joyful state of mind. If you've never tested your green thumb, plant some bulbs or herbs. Go to a baseball game and act as if you know exactly what's happening. Put a fake tattoo on your forearm. Check out the expressions on those you love and those you don't.

Step out of your routine. Do something out of the ordinary. Conspire with a friend to catch a matinee . . . in the middle of a workday! Take yourself out for dinner and order breakfast. Let your children get you ready for bed. Try to juggle in front of someone you know. Sing at the top of your lungs when you're driving or washing your hair.

practice

These things consistently bring me joy:

1. _____

   _____

2. _____

   _____

3. _____

   _____

The last time I laughed like there was no tomorrow was when:

1. _____

   _____

2. _____

_____

3. _____

_____

I can cultivate and invite fun into my life by:

1. _____

_____

2. _____

_____

3. _____

_____

affirm

I'm no longer constrained by stress and sorrow and can focus more clearly on what's really important.

When I replenish my fun jar, I

_____

_____

Create a Mentoring Squad

Those who trust us, educate us.
—George Eliot, *Daniel Deronda* (1874)

ask

1. What could I learn from my peers?
2. In an ideal world, who would be my mentors?
3. Would I be more comfortable in a formal mentoring relationship or one that is more casual and not as structured (scheduled meeting, written expectations, etc.)?
4. Is it necessary for me to have a lot in common with my mentor/mentee?
5. Would I ever feel threatened by a mentor/mentee?
6. Would I be a good mentor?
7. What could I offer as a mentor?

Mentoring isn't what it used to be. Certainly, several years ago formal mentoring programs had not yet become popular, and, frankly, seeking out a mentor seemed a little intimidating. Today, though, the opportunities for mentoring are endless, which is good news if you're trying to turn the life you're living into the life you want.

Old-style mentoring usually worked best by hooking up a longstanding successful employee with a bright-eyed newcomer. These days, though, it's not unusual for mentors and mentees to be the same age. You don't have to limit yourself to one person, either. The new school for mentoring says that it's okay, even preferable, to create a mentoring squad—a cadre of teachers and supporters who can help you tackle problems, share experiences, and provide steady encouragement. A mentor who recognizes your potential can mean the difference between confronting a challenge and giving up. Marika Flatt, national media director for a literary publicity firm, says her first mentoring experience was successful, in part, because her mentor could see how determined Marika was to learn about and improve her craft. "My first mentor was a female executive producer at a television station where I worked as a teen reporter in high school and college," she says. "She recognized my love for reporting and spurred me along. Later, when I was searching for a job after college, she recommended that I join the Association for Women in Communications. I attended my first happy-hour networking event and was given a job lead the following day by someone I met there, and I'm still at the job today." Today, Marika carries on that tradition by mentoring three colleagues.

A successful mentoring relationship should be based on trust, chemistry, and comfort. These qualities will help you ask questions and share information with more ease. You'll want to seek out mentors who are good listeners and will challenge you to take certain risks. If you hook up with a colleague or a supervisor, share information about your career with caution, especially if your mentors work for competing companies. You wouldn't want to jeopardize a relationship (or your company's bottom line) by sharing information that's proprietary.

Don't be afraid to walk away from a mentoring relationship that isn't working out. Some connections are not meant to last, and if you hang on too long you could lose interest in mentoring altogether. Consider these alliances as you might a friendship—you need to click on a personal level. And remember that no matter how strong the relationship becomes, you must always be the author of your dreams. Don't expect a mentor to fill in the blanks. And since we often learn by teaching what we don't know, think of your role in a mentoring squad as double-sided; you can be a mentor and be mentored at the same time.

As you assemble your mentoring squad make sure you are secure in your knowledge of self. It's fine to emulate others and set high expectations for yourself, but it's wrong and unrealistic to take on the precise qualities and characteristics of another person no matter how much you admire her. Mentoring should enhance your growth and development—not chip away at your character. Also, try not to think of mentoring as a fad—something you'll try, grow tired of, and finally abandon. Instead, take the long view and give yourself—and others—the chance to succeed.

experiment

Do it yourself. Some of the most successful mentoring programs are the ones that start because one person sees a need. As Tiffany Hoffine, a former audit manager at Deloitte & Touche (D&T) in Atlanta, moved up the career ladder, she found fewer and fewer prospective mentors. So, in 1998, Tiffany helped launch the company's first external mentoring program. D&T women are matched with talented, high-ranking, and high-powered women in the Atlanta business community. What makes this program so exciting is how each group is assembled: About five or six external mentors are matched with four women at D&T. The groups meet each quarter to talk about a variety of topics, some more general such as management styles, work/life balance, and diversity. Other discussions are more sensitive and focus on issues such as personnel. "The group dynamic makes it possible for me and my colleagues to mentor each other," says Tiffany, who has since moved on to Elite Financial Staffing. "The learning becomes exponential." If you see the need for such a program, like Tiffany, take the initiative and do it yourself, and watch the magic of women helping one another unfold and blossom. Don't forget to survey the group from time to time to gauge its effectiveness.

Hold confidentiality in the highest regard. A mentoring relationship can't be successful without confidentiality. For example, you need to know that whatever you say about a supervisor or a business idea won't be repeated. If you can't speak in a safe environment, you're not likely to learn or teach very much or very well.

Differentiate between mentor and coach. A mentor is not a coach. Unlike a coach, whom you pay to help you further your goals, a mentor acts as an adviser. A coach may ask you specific questions about where you want to go and help you determine what you need to get there. But don't expect a mentor to necessarily ask the questions or know your needs. Ann Latendresse, an executive with Great Clips, a hair salon franchise with headquarters in Minneapolis, says, "You have to be prepared to know what you want and what you need. Once I was able to articulate my needs, my mentor consistently challenged me, but I didn't rely on her to figure out what I wanted."

Mix and mismatch. It may be more comfortable and less threatening to align yourself with a like-minded mentor, someone with whom you have a lot in common or whose experience matches what you'd like to achieve. It's probably more challenging, however, to hook yourself up with someone who's different. Remember that the idea isn't to clone yourself into your mentor; the key is to learn from as many sources as possible. Often we learn the most from those who have completely different points of view. Valerie, who works in production management at a well-known fashion house, recognizes the importance of staying connected with people from various departments. "You don't have to know the science or each piece of someone's job," she says, "but you have to respect their knowledge. We may not do the wear testing, fit approval, or materials procurement, but we need to know how those functions fall into place so that we can deliver our products on time and assure customer satisfaction. This is something I try to impart to my assistant in my role as a mentor."

Set creative schedules. Consider meeting in a variety of locations at various times. A Sunday brunch instead of the usual after-work meeting can add a whimsical note; a potluck dinner at someone's home could be the perfect setting for a relaxing and fun meeting.

practice

In the past, I have admired the following people because:

1. _____

_____

2. _____

_____

3. _____

_____

A mentoring squad could help me:

1. _____

_____

2. _____

_____

3. _____

_____

I could be a good mentor by doing the following:

1. _____

_____

2. _____

_____

3. _____

_____

affirm

I am totally committed to being challenged by others who are willing to share what they know.

When I create my mentoring squad, I

_____

_____

Practice Forgiveness

Forgiveness is the economy of the heart. . . .
Forgiveness saves expense of anger, the cost
of hatred, the waste of spirits.
—Hannah More, "Christianity a Practical Principle,"
Practical Piety (1811)

ask

1. Do I wait for others to apologize?
2. How many times have I squandered an opportunity because I could not forgive?
3. Have I turned my inability to forgive into a habit?
4. What will it take for me to give up unrealistic expectations?
5. Can I imagine the peace that will come over me when I practice forgiveness?
6. Am I able to forgive myself?
7. If I could practice forgiveness, could I more easily turn the life I'm living into the life I want?

If you hold on to grudges for too long, the chances for integrating the life you're living into the life you want grow slim. Hanging on to grudges means you're concentrating on all the wrong things—past experiences that have no use on your path today. Instead of looking forward, you're fixated on something that's over. If you're still angry with a boss who never stood up for you, acknowledge your frustrations and give yourself permission to move on. Otherwise you'll continue to give this person power. If a parent forbade you from traveling abroad in high school, start planning your itinerary today. Even if the people you forgive aren't even remotely connected to your dreams, you will still discover a sense of release and serenity. The negative energy you previously spent on worry and unresolved conflicts will be replaced by a positive force that can be channeled into your efforts to wish, dream, and do.

Practicing forgiveness does not mean that old wounds will miraculously heal or that everything in your future will suddenly fall into place. It will help you, however, to become more receptive to moments that hold promise, hope, and joy. Fred Luskin, Ph.D., a psychologist and researcher at Stanford University, has studied the effects of forgiveness for years. "It's important to practice forgiveness so you don't prejudice your present experience," says Luskin, director and cofounder of the Stanford University Forgiveness Project. "Unresolved hurt and anger prevents you from being flexible and adaptive and ultimately less capable of generating an optimal response."

Sometimes the stuff we carry around from year to year affects us in subtle yet insidious ways. An old experience and the accompanying response can embed themselves in your memory and in the way you conduct yourself from day to day—your language, your mannerisms, your style. Old offenses can also come to life as if they happened just moments ago. "Every time you're reminded of someone or something that caused you emotional distress, it's another reminder of your helplessness," says Luskin, who also teaches forgiveness classes.

When we feel helpless we play the victim. It's a form of surrender that keeps us tethered to wounded feelings. Practicing forgiveness, however, shifts the focus, so that instead of dwelling on the people who have hurt us in the past, we turn away from the experience and replenish the painful memories with moments with joy. As Luskin, author of *Forgive for Good*, says, "A life well lived is your best revenge."

experiment

Forgive in absentia. In most cases, we equate forgiveness with some kind of confrontation. However, forgiving someone can be just as effective when offered in the absence of an apology. First, if you wait for someone to apologize, you could be waiting forever. Second, the expectation of an apology puts someone else in control. Forgiveness is a state of mind that requires no intervention.

Forgive with a letter. Consider writing your forgiveness. You can pen a letter to send, keep, or destroy. If you do send it, be sure to be prepared for any consequences. You might get a phone call, a letter, or absolutely nothing. You can fill a journal and squeeze out every injustice that's made a much-too-permanent place in your soul. That the words stay on the page won't dilute their potency. It is the energy you put toward transforming years of emotion into a readable language that is important. When journaling your forgiveness, you call the shots and you make the rules. Be truthful; this will help you understand who you are and why forgiving will heal and help you.

Forgive yourself. Don't hold yourself hostage to past indiscretions. Set yourself free and leave behind assumptions that you're not good enough. For many years Robin had trouble forgiving herself for every wrong thing she'd ever done. "I felt like one long continuous mistake, as if the next wrongdoing was right around the corner no matter what I did," she says. "This diminished my capacity to forgive others. I began to catalog grudge after grudge. It made me feel sick inside until I finally decided to forgive myself. Once I made that decision, forgiving others became easier." We all need to be corrected and that's absolutely okay. Yet, you can improve and forgive yourself *at the very same time*. You mustn't wait until you've reached "perfection," as if you'll never do something wrong again. We'll always blow it from time to time, and perfection is no good anyway. Who ever learned anything by being perfect?

practice

Practicing forgiveness will help me replace anger and fear with:

1. _____

_____

2. _____

_____

3. _____

_____

When I forgive others, I change in the following positive ways:

1. _____

_____

2. _____

3. _____

_____

_____

As I learn to forgive more easily, I can turn the life I'm living into the life I want by:

1. _____

_____

2. _____

_____

3. _____

_____

affirm

Forgiving others enables me to accept people for who they are, not for what I'd like them to be.

When I practice forgiveness, I

_____

_____

Perform Mistake Magic

*There's nothing final about a mistake, except its
being taken as final.*
—Phyllis Bottome, "The Plain Case,"
Strange Fruit (1928)

ask

1. Do I admit my mistakes?
2. How accepting am I of other people's mistakes?
3. Do I forgive myself when I've made a mistake or do I feel
   unworthy?
4. Do my mistakes bring me to a standstill or do they help
   me move on?
5. Do my mistakes define who I am?
6. Is my life richer because of the mistakes I've made?
7. Can I achieve my dreams without ever making mistakes?

We all make mistakes. That's what makes us human. Yet, our
culture doesn't always embrace the notion of openly acknowledging our wrongdoings. Generally speaking, we're not rewarded for
the mistakes we make. But our mistakes offer a reward, if we
choose to see them as a lesson to be learned instead of a source of
shame.

Think of Jane, a free-spirited artist who, for years, worked behind a desk in order to meet the mortgage and put shoes on her kids' feet. One day she missed a major deadline. The next month she was downsized out of a job and privately attributed her loss to a former scheduling slip-up. Temporary financial hardship followed, but a year later, doing the work of her dreams, she said, "Missing that deadline was the best mistake I ever made."

One of my favorite mistakes is the historical "blunder" made so many years ago in the labs of 3M. Researcher Spencer Silver developed a temporary adhesive that, in its initial form, could not be brought to market. Later, another researcher, Art Fry, remembered the substance when he became frustrated by the slippery paper bookmarks he used in his hymnal to mark certain songs. The rest, they say, is history, and today, if you're like me, you rely on the convenience and ease of 3M's Post-it Notes.

experiment

Give your mistakes a deadline. Next time you make a mistake, give yourself a short and specific period of time during which you will allow yourself to think about what's happened, note a lesson, and then move on. You'll move forward more quickly and leave the bad feelings behind.

Get unstuck. Are you too attached to a not-so-great idea? Sticking with a mediocre idea may feel more comfortable than trying a new, and possibly riskier, idea. Establish some distance between you and this comfort zone and you might experience a drop in the number of mistakes you make.

Seek support. Seek the support of people who love you for who you are, not for what you do. Next time you say the wrong thing or forget to come through, tell someone that you blew it. More than likely this person will share a story of her own and you'll both be vying for the blunder-of-the-year award.

Look at history. Think back to a time when a mistake led you toward a more enriching path, one that you might not have taken had your error never occurred. Think not only of the outcome but also of the feelings that accompanied your efforts to work things through. Think of the strength you gained by flexing your psychic muscles and coming out more solid, more spirited, more of who you were meant to be.

practice

When I make a mistake, I respond by:

1. _____

_____

2. _____

_____

3. _____

_____

Instead of feeling guilty or ashamed, I will:

1. _____

_____

2. _____

_____

3. _____

_____

As I wish, dream, and do, my mistakes will help me:

1. _____

_____

2. _____

_____

3. _____

_____

affirm

Once I have turned them into lessons, my mistakes become assets, so that I am always getting better.

When I practice mistake magic, I

_____

_____

Love Yourself from the Inside Out

There is an applause superior to that of the multitude—one's own.
　　—Elizabeth Elton Smith, *The Three Eras of Woman's Life* (1836)

ask

1. Do I speak well of myself to others?
2. Do I embrace the concept of self-love easily?
3. What are some ways that I demonstrate self-respect?
4. Would I ever send myself a valentine?
5. Can I be disappointed in myself and practice self-love at the same time?
6. Can I forgive myself for my transgressions?
7. Am I willing to make the effort involved in loving the person I am?

Do you ever stand up and cheer for *you?* Do you remember to give yourself gold stars? Do you count yourself as one of the people you love the most? You must be willing to regard yourself with unconditional love.

Loving yourself unconditionally means that you *stay with yourself* no matter what. You may be a blockbuster success story waiting to happen, but unless you love and respect your heart, soul, and spirit, your efforts will always carry a trace of self-doubt. Not only will that prevent you from reaching your potential, but your lack of self-love will be evident to the people around you. Telling people you don't deserve something or that you never get anything right is what they'll remember. Writer Pam Grout used to think that her success depended on where she lived. "I used to feel inferior that I live in a small town in Kansas rather than in New York City or on the West Coast," she says. "But over time I realized that I had an opportunity to be a self-starter. There are no literary agents in my town or big-time publishers or anyone else I could lean on. What I did was up to me. That gave me tremendous power." Instead of feeling—and act-ing—undeserving, as if she hadn't done enough, Pam recognized that she *is* enough and *good* enough as well regardless of where she lives. It's true that to love others you must first love yourself. It's also essential to love yourself before you can accept love from someone else.

experiment

Listen to your language. Do you ever speak to yourself in a tone you wouldn't use with a best friend? If you're hearing too many harsh words from within, it's time to stop. You can't love yourself from the inside out if your inner critic always has the floor. You may not be able to push her off the stage each and every time she appears, but you can reel her in from time to time with one simple phrase: "That's enough."

Think well of yourself. Just as you can quiet your inner critic, you can turn up the volume for your biggest fan. She's the one who says things like, "You're doing the best you can"; "I learn something new from every experience"; and "I did it! I actually, finally did it!" Give her as much air time as you can spare. Using a fresh pad of Post-its, jot down as many affirmations as you can think of and then, one by one, place them where you're most likely to see them—on your phone, refrigerator (inside and out), steering wheel, computer, above the light switch in your kitchen. For starters, try these: "I look beautiful today"; "I'm good at————"; "My hard work is paying off"; "I trust the wisdom from within"; "I am good enough"; and so on.

Don't give yourself away. Why do we give things away? Sometimes we grow out of something—a shirt, a sweater, a pair of pants. Maybe an old serving dish doesn't match your new decor. You've read all the books on your shelf, so you donate them to the local hospital. What we keep, though, we hold dear. When you love yourself from the inside out, you vow to keep yourself. Don't give yourself away as if you've outgrown who you are. Your capacity to love yourself will grow as you grow, so hold on tight and keep it forever. Indeed, the love you give yourself will always be a perfect fit.

practice

In the past, I've put myself down with comments like:

1. _____

   _____

2. _____

   _____

3. _____

   _____

Sometimes I'm afraid to love myself because:

1. _____

_____

2. _____

_____

3. _____

_____

I'm learning that I can more easily love myself from the inside out by:

1. _____

_____

2. _____

_____

3. _____

_____

affirm

When I love myself from the inside out I stop longing for and seeking approval from others.

When I love myself from the inside out, I

_____

_____

Respond with Compassion

*Nobody likes having salt rubbed into their
wounds, even if it is the salt of the earth.*
—Rebecca West, "The Salt of the Earth,"
The Harsh Voice (1935)

ask

1. Am I compassionate toward myself, particularly if I've experienced a setback?
2. Can I respond with compassion even when frustration and anger are my initial feelings?
3. When I respond with compassion, do I ever feel resentful?
4. How can I add a little more compassion to my daily routines?
5. Am I willing to reexperience an old hurt in order to help a friend feel better?
6. Can I put my needs and problems aside if someone needs my compassion?
7. How is my journey enhanced when I respond to others with compassion?

Reaching out to others with a kind word, a helpful hint, or some reassurance has a way of coming full circle. Writer and speaker

Sandy Beckwith believes that each time she extends her hand to someone, she will be repaid in kind. She can't schedule or predict when that might occur, but she is convinced that what goes around still comes around. "Why shouldn't I help someone else? It's always come back to me," she says. "Maybe I have the ideal 'helpful people corner,'" she adds, referring to the feng shui component that associates compassion with the placement of certain objects in a room.

Lenore Weiss Baigelman, an architect and coauthor of *Feng Shui Principles for Building and Remodeling*, explains that the ancient Chinese believed that if people showed concern for their guests, the occupants would in turn be cared for by others. "The newer school of feng shui, the pyramid school, puts the emphasis on the group versus the individual," says Lenore. "In other words, if you express compassion to others, people will be more compassionate toward you."

Compassion means "to feel with," to actually imagine yourself in another person's uncomfortable, too small, totally out of fashion (or fabulously sublime) shoes. When you stop and put yourself in a place where you can practically feel someone else's anguish, you can react—truthfully and sincerely—with compassion. Instead of saying, "Oh, it's no big deal," or, "You'll get over it," those who respond compassionately are willing to experience the pain as if it were their own. If we all cultivate compassion, each of our individual journeys will be easier and more fruitful. For example, if you're managing a team that's encountered trouble with a project, withhold your criticism and instead attempt to see the problem from your group's point of view. By combining your expertise with another perspective, you're more likely to discover a better solution.

experiment

Start close to home. Cultivating compassion toward yourself enhances your ability to do the same with others. Being hard on yourself may offer a few short-term benefits, but in the long run the kindness you extend to yourself will naturally find its way to others.

Respond with compassion, not control. Sometimes it's hard to refrain from telling other people what to do. But that's the last thing to do when a friend or colleague is feeling down. Generally, most people want to be listened to and validated. Sharing your experiences and telling them that you understand is often enough.

Cultivate compassion wherever you go. Expand your capacity to respond with compassion by reaching out to people you don't even know. Offer to help the stranger who tripped beside you on the sidewalk. Tell the forlorn-looking cashier to have a wonderful day. Gently smile at and assist the woman who inadvertently creates an avalanche of falling apples in the produce section of your grocery store.

practice

In the past, I haven't always responded with compassion, mostly because:

1. _____

_____

2. _____

_____

3. _____

_____

Responding with compassion brings me peace in the following ways:

1. _____

_____

2. _____

_____

3. _____

_____

This week, I'm going be more compassionate toward:

1. _____

_____

2. _____

_____

3. _____

_____

affirm

Listening and speaking with compassion is like coating my heart and soul with a layer of understanding.

When I respond with compassion, I

_____

_____

Simplify When You Can

*Simplicity is an acquired taste. Mankind, left
free, instinctively complicates life.*
—Katharine Fullerton Gerould,
Modes and Morals (1920)

ask

1. How do I currently handle clutter?
2. What am I willing to do about it?
3. Is my plate always filled to the brim?
4. Am I overly dependent on e-mail, my cell phone, and call waiting?
5. How do I picture a simpler life?
6. Does clutter literally get in the way of my wishes and dreams?
7. Do my relationships ever prevent me from pursuing my dreams?

Several years ago the simplicity movement swept into our collective psyche. Most of the experts focused on *stuff*—household items like clothes and books that could be discarded (though some books should never be given away), products that we didn't need to buy in the first place, and of course the oppressive mountains of junk mail. Yet, despite our efforts to clean up, we're still drawn to circumstances and people that complicate rather than simplify our lives. It's as if simplifying and slowing down will cut our supply of oxygen or, at the very least, drain all of our reserves. Not surprisingly, though, it's the complexities that sap us of energy and, in the long run, prevent us from capturing our dreams. In many cases, it's best to simplify when you can.

Ironically, simplicity is hard work. You do have to clean up some, and you can't buy everything in sight. Sometimes you even have to say "no." All of this takes a certain resolve, a real commitment to clear out whatever is keeping your dreams out of reach. It's not always obvious, though. You may be so accustomed to cramming a lot into your day (or week) that the thought of cutting back just doesn't register. However, when we can peel away the nonessentials, we generally discover that our lives are easier, cleaner.

This is especially true as it relates to the people in your life. You may have lots of friends and/or acquaintances, but who's in your inner circle? Who supports your dreams? Examining your relationships may be painful, particularly when you discover that certain people limit your abilities to wish, dream, and do. Yet, once you're able to determine what's working, you'll be able to focus on the large and small moments that really matter.

I try to simplify whenever possible. Sometimes it's too late and I wonder, after the fact, why I turned a manageable situation into one that became unwieldy and stressful. But I'm learning. Fast. Because I can definitely see a correlation between simplifying when I can and integrating the life I'm living into the life I want. For example, if I know that driving carpool will put me into a deadline tailspin, I ask for help and promise to drive another time. If buying a bag of prewashed lettuce means that I'll eat a healthier lunch, then I'll do it. If declining an invitation for a girls-night-out means that I'm home with a kid who needs me, I'll do that, too. It's been a slow and deliberate process, but the results have been fulfilling and hopeful.

experiment

Make a decision and stick with it. Sometimes we accumulate too much stuff because we can't make a decision. "Oh, well, sure, I'll take it," you might say without even thinking. Or maybe you're waiting for some divine intervention to determine what you should throw away and what you should keep. If you're from the I-might-need-that-someday school of thought, stop giving the item so much power. If you haven't needed it by now, you probably can do without it.

Pay attention to your peccadilloes. What really, really bugs you? Call waiting? Too many magazines to read? Back-to-back meetings? Pay attention to what makes you want to scream. But instead of exploding, make a mental note to eliminate or at least minimize those pesky tyrannies. It's those weighty annoyances that may feel like obligations but in reality are extras that you can do without.

Read the Cliffs Notes. Not only is it inadvisable to get involved with too much, it is simply impossible. You will not perish if you don't read the daily paper from cover to cover. Read the headlines if you don't have time. You will be no less cultured if you miss the biggest art exhibit to come to town. Before you buy five of something in the latest fashion, ask yourself how your life will change if you absolutely, positively do without it.

Redefine and refine your relationships. This is a long-term and often ongoing process. If a relationship is painful for you, examine it closely and decide if your life would improve if you broke it off. Clearly, some relationships are permanent, but they can be helped. If you can't work it out yourself, seek professional help. Sometimes an objective point of view is all you need to reevaluate a relationship.

Draw a line between your past and this very moment. Your history is a part of who you are, but you don't have to bring it with you everywhere you go. Similarly, old wounds don't have to be reopened, especially if you can separate who you are today from the pain you left behind. Revisiting and overanalyzing the past can complicate your life to the point where you might forfeit the future. Learn from the past and bring the lessons with you. Keep the bad feelings where they belong: in an old place where you used to live.

practice

Sometimes I unnecessarily complicate matters by:

1. _____

_____

2. _____

_____

3. _____

_____

When I simplify certain areas of my life, I feel:

1. _____

_____

2. _____

_____

3. _____

_____

I will try to simplify the way I:

1. _____

_____

2. _____

_____

3. _____

_____

affirm

I worry less about what I don't have and focus more on what's right before my eyes.

Simplifying when I can allows me to

_____

_____

Yield to the Moment

The worst thing that can be said of a man [or woman] is that he [or she] did not pay attention.

—William Meredith

ask

1. Do I tend to let the moment go and then later regret it?
2. Do I make an effort to yield to the moment?
3. Can I live inside a moment and be prepared for whatever comes next?
4. Can I live in the moment even when it's painful?
5. Can I surrender to whim without worrying that I could be missing something more important?
6. Would the people I love the most say that I practice mindfulness?
7. Is spontaneity an important component in my efforts to wish, dream, and do?

When we yield to the moment we slide in beside it just as we might carefully guide a car into traffic. The stream of moving vehicles is like a current of moments, constantly sweeping us into life. Yet, with all this motion and speed, is it possible to capture and truly be with the moment? We get high marks for thinking ahead and being prepared, but some of us still struggle at times with our ability to be mindful of where we are right now. Maybe it's because we're waiting for the next big thing instead of enjoying what's right before our eyes. How can we operate with care *and* embrace spontaneity? Can we really learn to savor the smaller moments in life, the quiet and private moments when we aren't *doing* but simply *being*?

One way to test your mindfulness is to stop, look, and listen. Ask yourself, "What am I aware of right this minute?" Take deep breaths, look around, and really examine something as if you're seeing it for the first time. These are demonstrations of real mindfulness. Giving your undivided attention to someone puts you in the present moment as well. To successfully yield to the moment, you must be willing to relinquish your expectations. Instead of trying to calculate the effects of a particular situation, try to embrace and be satisfied by the moment alone, not for what it might mean in three months. Don't be surprised, though, by a moment's long shelf life. What brings you peace and serenity today could unexpectedly help you endure a difficult situation tomorrow. The memory alone can heal and restore when you need it most.

Yielding to the moment doesn't mean you have to leave behind an ordered life. Some of the freest spirits I know are the most organized people as well. Similarly, you don't have to completely clear your life of chaos in order to be present in the moment. Mindfulness comes from within. For Jodi Cohen, paying attention to the moment is essential to her craft. "I've been performing and teaching improvisation for nearly twenty years," she says. "What I love about improv as an art form is that it requires me to be present, to let go of any agenda, planning, and worries. It forces me to be in the moment and that's very liberating."

Rose Berman-Golubchick, an immigrant from Latvia, found that mindfulness enabled her to leave nursing in order to pursue another caring field. "I loved nursing but eventually I grew weary of illness," she says. "I tried to pay attention to what before felt natural—my calling, really—but was becoming uncomfortable and negative. I still wanted to care for people, but I needed to be around wellness, not sickness. I had to pay attention to a voice I hadn't heard before. I became very interested in health and beauty and was drawn to the way certain treatments can revive and rejuvenate." Today she owns a full-service salon where clients flock to reduce stress, increase their resilience, and revitalize their minds and bodies. "I'll always be in a healing profession. It is my nature to care for people. At one time in my life that meant patients who needed to get well. Today it's people who need to relax."

experiment

Live inside the moment. Instead of watching a moment happen, step inside and become a part of it. Just because you don't put the moment into words doesn't mean you can't experience and fold it into your life. Once you learn how to live inside the moment, you lose the desire to control it, and that can make for a much more serene way of life.

Yield to moments of varying size. Some moments are large and splash into our lives with unbreakable force. Other moments are small and quiet, slipping into our consciousness with little fanfare. But both are significant and can alter our lives in ways we might not expect. Being present to a wide range of moments will help you minimize the possibility of missing even one.

Be alone with your moments. Some moments draw on every ounce of your ability to concentrate. But distractions can interrupt the flow, so that instead of capturing the moment, it breaks apart and disappears. Don't be afraid to pour your focus into the present moment. In some cases, the moment will temporarily spirit you away from others. But don't confuse your solitariness with being standoffish or impolite. Sometimes we learn best through independent study.

practice

I'm beginning to think that maybe I can be more present when:

1. _____

_____

2. _____

_____

3. _____

_____

Sometimes remembering a peaceful moment from my past helps me:

1. _____

_____

2. _____

_____

3. _____

_____

When I'm in between the past and the future, my "now" looks like:

1. _____

_____

2. _____

_____

3. _____

_____

affirm

I string together each moment so that the strand of my life becomes stronger with each passing day.

When I yield to the moment, I

_____

_____

~ week 48 ~

Take Care of Yourself

Health is not a condition of matter, but of Mind.

—Mary Baker Eddy, *Science and Health* (1875)

ask

1. Is it hard for me to say "no"?
2. Do I frequently take on more than I can handle?
3. Am I regularly overcome by stress and anxiety?
4. Do I equate good health with sustenance and inspiration?
5. Do I pay attention to my spirit?
6. How do I practice self-care now?
7. What can I do right now to feel a little better?

Amid your hot pursuit of wishes and dreams, you are likely, at one point or another, to shortchange what should always be at the top of your list: your physical and spiritual health. Without it, the path leading to your goals will be littered with aches and pains, prescriptions, even hospital stays. It's funny how the illnesses that knock us flat—bad colds, the flu, a broken bone—get our full attention and force us to slow down, regroup, and give ourselves time to heal. Yet, the quieter forms of malaise such as stress and heart disease, while just as serious, are too often overlooked and put in a corner somewhere to be "dealt with later." That's a dicey business and a practice that can derail your efforts to wish, dream, and do.

Why is self-care so illusive anyway? Most of us are taught early on how to take care of ourselves. We learn the basics of hygiene and usually we know how to do a load of laundry by the time we're eighteen. And as often as we hear friends and family say, "Take care of yourself," mastering the skills required to fulfill our needs is no simple task. Maybe that's the problem—perhaps we view self-care as just one more item on our to-do lists.

If maintaining a healthy lifestyle seems too burdensome, it's time to create a program of your own, even if it's loose and somewhat fluid. The objective is to find ways to practice self-care that *feel good*. Once you accomplish that, you'll have the reserves you need to engage in the hard work of your dreams. If you need to change a behavior, you're likely to bend more easily. If you need to negotiate for a more reasonable schedule, you'll have the psychic energy required to reassign tasks and responsibilities. If you need to stop what you're doing to care for a sick child or parent, you'll have the strength to give to others without making yourself ill.

Practicing self-care is for your current well-being, not just for your long-term health. Sometimes we need to take care of ourselves in the moment, too. Andrea Fulcher, director of revenue analysis at Marriott's Marco Island Resort, takes care of herself by setting aside two hours each morning from five to seven o'clock. "I use the time to exercise and sort through my day," she says. "We work ten-hour days and that uninterrupted time gives me a chance to get grounded and prepared for what's ahead. I manage rates and revenues and demand in what today is an uncertain economy. That puts pressure on me, but by fueling up each morning I'm able to put my best self forward."

Some people say they forget to eat lunch (not I!) or never get enough sleep. Nurturing and soothing activities may seem out of reach or intended for people "more in touch" with their bodies. Comfort is viewed as an infrequent treat, a state of mind reserved for those with more time on their hands. As convincing as it all sounds, however, you can choose to believe otherwise. Each statement above is negative and self-defeating and will never help you turn what you want into what is yours. As you fold self-care behaviors into your life, make a commitment to curb and, ultimately, release thoughts that are incompatible with your well-being.

experiment

Say "yes" when a friend asks you to come out and play. My friend Sallyan, who provided inspiration for this chapter, periodically puts together irresistible grown-up play dates. That she knows her way around Chicago is certainly an advantage, but it is her generous spirit that I truly cherish. Maybe you're asked out to dinner or a cousin wants you to join her for dinner this Friday night. Before you say "no," imagine the soothing effects of letting someone lift you up from the intensity of your hard work.

Subscribe to one health-related magazine. I know how overwhelming a stack of magazines can be, but you might be surprised by what you can learn by reading just one health-oriented title per month. Sections often include shortcut strategies for cutting some of the stress out of your life, easy recipes that are healthy and taste good, first-person accounts that will help you realize that you're not alone in your quest for bringing comfort to your life, and other news that you can add to your self-care arsenal.

Create a spiritual multivitamin. Next time you're near a bottle of multivitamins (hopefully, you've got one in your kitchen or somewhere else in your home), think about how you can create your custom-made spiritual supplement. Include activities and states of mind such as five minutes of peace, a fifteen-minute walk outside no matter what, a small piece of your all-time favorite chocolate, or a long-distance call to an old friend. Combine 150 milligrams of discovering something new about yourself, 250 milligrams of celebrating a recent victory—large or small—and other ingredients likely to restore your physical and emotional well-being. Take just one tablet daily. Remember, too, that nurturing yourself takes practice. This is a learned behavior, but once you've got the basics, the rest is a cakewalk, or perhaps I should say a high-fiber-muffin walk.

Set a trap for self-sabotaging behaviors. How many times have you heard about someone intent upon succeeding, only to set herself up for failure time and time again? Sound familiar? Gloria, a successful woman I know, finally found her calling after recognizing and accepting her aversion to math. "I was a bank vice president filling out loan applications and I couldn't figure out where to put the decimal point," she says. Gloria reveled in the interactions she had with customers and other employees but withered when she had to crunch numbers. "Suddenly I'd been thrown into a left-brain environment. I took remedial math courses, but nothing changed. I even used to sing a song every morning—'I don't want to go to work, I don't want to go to work.'" Eventually, Gloria left banking, but not until she'd put in ninety part-time days at another bank. After that she left the industry completely and vowed that she would never go back to something she didn't like.

Practice saying "sorry," "no," and "not at this time." We're so good at saying "yes," "sure," and, "I'd be happy to." If we say "no," we risk experiencing that impenetrable pause when someone, a little stunned, attempts to absorb your unconventional response. Yet if you say "yes" too often, you won't be doing enough for yourself.

practice

Sometimes it's hard to take care of myself because:

1. _____

_____

2. _____

_____

3. _____

_____

In the past, when I've practiced self-care, I've felt:

1. _____

_____

2. _____

_____

3. _____

_____

Today, I can start taking care of myself by:

1. _____

_____

2. _____

_____

3. _____

_____

affirm

It is my birthright to feel as good as I can.

When I take care of myself, I

_____

_____

Put Your Faith to Work

Faith hasn't got no eyes, but she' long-legged.
—Zora Neale Hurston, *Jonah's Gourd Vine* (1934)

ask

1. How much faith do I have in my wishes and dreams?
2. Do I ever lose faith? When?
3. When do I rely on my faith?
4. How have I related to faith in the past?
5. Does having faith make anything possible?
6. What does faith look like for me on a typical day?
7. Can I really put my faith to work?

Putting your faith to work may sound a little contradictory. After all, how can you formalize a concept that is by definition unknown, even mystical? How can something so personal be turned into a strategy, a method for creating realities out of hopes and dreams? Having faith doesn't necessarily make life easier, but it does help us put one foot in front of the other, particularly on those days when the future seems bleak and uncharitable. In many ways, faith moves upon instinct, especially as it passes through murky darkness. Faith also is a teacher, instructing and encouraging us to trust the process *and* the outcome. Faith helps us distinguish between what we can influence and what occurs regardless of our input. Putting your faith to work is about getting up each morning knowing that whatever you do has a purpose—a higher purpose—and is part of a larger plan that will help you turn the life you're living into the life you want.

For Cathy Brandell, asking for faith establishes the direction for her day. "Once I wake up, I sit quietly and wait for the light with a cup of hot tea," she says. "Then I thank God for his blessings from the previous day—good or bad—and then ask for his or her good graces for the new day. If I don't ask, I won't get, and for me, faith is in the asking and knowing that whatever happens occurs for a reason." Indeed, Cathy put her faith to work one morning and by the afternoon had replaced the income from one former client to a new customer. "I'd been with a client for nine years as a marketing consultant but had trained everyone so well that ultimately I wasn't needed anymore. I realized that and told them I had to move on. I was concerned about the money but I had tremendous faith that I'd repeat the experience with something new and different. I went from something totally different—actuary work—to a title company with virtually no interruption in my income."

We may be unable to see what's ahead, but we *can* use all our might to get there. Much of the energy that propels us forward comes from faith. Faith is like a renewable fuel—it gets recycled each time it's used. So, the more faith we put into the universe, the farther it travels. And as our collective faith blazes a trail into the world, something extraordinary occurs: We become more receptive to whatever comes our way. Instead of being afraid of what we don't know, we replace our fear with faith.

experiment

Give your faith room to stretch. Don't restrict your faith to the possibility of one miracle. Faith is not about winning the lottery or getting the part or securing the loan. Faith is more about stretching your beliefs across a wide spectrum so that you can remain receptive to all possibilities.

Welcome the miracles. Your faith does not discriminate between miracles and unfavorable situations. Your faith is a force that welcomes both. When miracles occur, embrace them and let their magic influence all that you do. Think of each extraordinary event as a response from the universe to your unwavering faith.

Tap in to your supportive resources. If your faith is floundering, check in with the people who know you best and can reignite your faith with just a few encouraging words. *Their faith in you* can also be put to work.

Rely on a higher power. Many of us are pretty good at heaping a lot of responsibility upon ourselves. Engendering a sense of faith gives us a chance to unload some of that burden. As you wish, dream, and do, try to rely on a higher power that might very well help you handle what's incredibly challenging, mildly annoying, and wonderfully overwhelming. In this context, think of your faith as a spiritual baggage handler, a carrier of all your hopes and dreams.

practice

Currently, my faith is being tested by:

1. _____

_____

2. _____

_____

3. _____

_____

I can call on my faith to help me:

1. _____

_____

2. _____

_____

3. _____

_____

I can bring faith into my daily routine by:

1. _____

_____

2. _____

_____

3. _____

_____

affirm

I trust what I know yet remain open and flexible to what will happen next.

When I put my faith to work, I

_____

_____

Become Your Own Center of Gravity

If you are not your own agent, you are some one else's.

—Alice Molloy, *In Other Words* (1973)

ask

1. How frequently do I compare myself to others?
2. On what occasions am I envious of other people?
3. What do they have that I don't have?
4. Do I generally accept who I am?
5. For the most part, do I do things because I want to or because they seem like the thing to do?
6. Do I try to please others at the expense of my own well-being?
7. What am I avoiding when I focus too much on what someone else is doing/accomplishing/celebrating?

Not long ago I read an article about a VIP whose name is synonymous with American royalty. The writer characterized him with God-like terms, though behind-the-scenes descriptions evoked a more down-to-earth image. Still, I was struck by the notion that even in a typical office environment this famous person became everyone else's center of gravity. Certainly, some people seen from a distance, and in person, seem larger than life. But if you intend to wish, dream, and do with authenticity, you must become your own center of gravity.

Although our culture is set up to laud the success of others, it is imperative that you never lose sight of your major and minor accomplishments. When we allow others to be our center of gravity, we neglect our own efforts. Plus, we forget that even those larger-than-life figures have their demons to deal with. Without seeing the entire picture, we imagine that their paths are smooth and struggle-free. We know deep down, however, that most people's paths are rarely free of trouble. That's when we make the distinction between what we imagine and what we know is true. Everyone struggles, so why not focus on what we *can* influence—our own lives?

Nick Graham of the Joe Boxer company knows the importance of influencing what he can. Working at a company that believes "fun is an everyday experience" allows Nick to embrace his work with creativity and individuality, which probably explains his job title: Chief Underpant Officer & Lord of Balls. "Our philosophy and products are both unusual and memorable and I wanted my title to reflect that. It gets people's attention, which ultimately helps me get closer to my professional goals," he says.

In many cases, other people become our center of gravity because it's easier to inhale someone else's success than to work toward and breathe in our own. However, being a spectator has its risks, too. You may be out of the arena and safe from injury, but you sacrifice achieving your own hard-won victories. Still, it's possible to break free of this behavior. First, decide once and for all to reclaim the energy you spend on someone else's good fortune, fame, or whatever, and apply it to your efforts. You may not even know where to start, but make the commitment anyway and treat yourself as if you are, indeed, the star of your life. Next, you must engage in the kind of thinking and doing that engenders self-acceptance. That might mean taking a taking a good, hard look at your warts, bad hair days, and everything else you're made of. Once you can accept the good with the bad—and whatever lies in between—you're in a much better position to be yourself *for yourself.* Don't try to impress anyone or puff yourself up only to become deflated when you can't hold it in anymore. When we try too hard to be who we're not, it always shows and sometimes quite badly. Once you become comfortable with who you are—and that could take a while—you won't need to rely on others for validation. You will discover that no one else can offer what you have to give the world.

experiment

Avoid the quicksand. Allowing others to be our center of gravity is like pouring out our own supply of quicksand. It is a no-win situation. Inevitably we neglect our potential by focusing too much on someone else's success. We get stuck. The other person's life becomes more attractive than ours and we simply stop trying. In the short term, wishing and dreaming based on someone else's life is easier. However, you're nowhere near the point where you can begin to turn the life you're living into the life you want.

Stay true to your values. You may be enamored with someone's financial success and fame (or whatever else seems appealing), but what happens when you begin to notice something unsavory about her values? What if she's conducting herself in a way that doesn't align with your moral code? Staying true to your values will keep you grounded, so that you have only to look within to find your center of gravity.

Stay strong as you migrate back home. If you're human, you've certainly gravitated toward people whom you admire and want to emulate. They make us happy and help us feel good about ourselves. But when they become your center of gravity, you tend to forget your soul. Once you recognize where you're going and you begin to move back "home," stay strong. You may doubt your instincts and wonder what you might be giving up. But it's still okay to return home, especially when your heart and spirit are beckoning you.

practice

Sometimes I set myself up for failure / disappointment when I pay too much attention to the way others:

1. _____

_____

2. _____

_____

3. _____

_____

I can become my own center of gravity by spending more time:

1. _____

_____

2. _____

_____

3. _____

_____

By going deeper into myself, I am discovering that:

1. _____

_____

2. _____

_____

3. _____

_____

affirm

I listen to my own voice and celebrate what's unique about me.

When I become my own center of gravity, I

_____

_____

~ week 51 ~

Live with the Distractions

*We can never catch up with life. . . . We shall
always be eating the soft part of our melting
ice and meanwhile the nice hard part is rapidly
melting too.*
—M. P. Follett, *Creative Experience* (1924)

ask

1. Why do I think of distractions as something bad?
2. Is it easier to complain about my chaos than it is to admit that some disorder is inevitable?
3. Am I willing to admit that some things, especially distractions, are out of my control?
4. Are my distractions feeding my workaholic tendencies?
5. Am I afraid of how I might feel if I don't have any distractions?
6. Do I know the difference between distractions that simply keep me busy and those that truly need to get done?
7. Do I ever busy myself with tasks so that I can avoid the hard work of my dreams?

When your distractions turn into excuses, you move further and further from doing what is meaningful. You may even begin to look at everything with an eye that sees only unfinished projects, the kind that nip at your heels and keep you up at night. But just because a task (or two or three) awaits your attention doesn't mean that you can't pursue your dreams as well. If you're always waiting to finish your have-to tasks before you attend to your dreams, you'll never get a sense of what it feels like to actually complete a project, to have done something well. And your dreams will constantly get pushed aside. That's why you need to find a way to live with your distractions. If you want to take on more clients for your coaching business *and* maintain the freedom you need to manage your home, set realistic and specific goals for both parts of your life. Don't minimize one area at the expense of the other. Writer Pam Grout says that even when you're distracted you can still think about what is possible. "You can be thinking about doing great things while you're taking your daughter's temperature or even while you're lying next to her watching an old movie."

To truly live in harmony with your distractions, you must be willing to do some things one at a time. It's true that some responsibilities can't wait. But others can be shifted around if you're willing to make certain decisions about what's really important and what can wait. For many—whether you run a big, successful company or are just starting out with the seed of an idea—housework is a huge, collective distraction. Walk from one corner of your home to another on a particularly messy day and you're likely to make frequent stops to bend, pick up, and put away. Your quick stroll from one room to another suddenly turns into a full-blown tour of duty. You may have gone to fetch a pen and spent a half hour straightening up. That's not living with the distractions; it's more like living under their rule.

This week, try to look at your distractions with a new and discerning eye. Put your distractions into perspective by prioritizing and separating the really important stuff from everything else. Carry a clipboard in your mind's eye and take mental notes of the situation. If it helps, imagine wearing a white lab coat, too. Remember that right now you're an observer, recording and then later absorbing the data. If your inner critic drops in, ask her to speak quietly because right now you're very busy.

experiment

Remove the weight of the world. Contrary to what you might believe, the sky will not fall if you stop trying to do everything. The world will continue to spin and somehow, some way, you will accomplish what needs to get done. In fact, it's okay to pare down your activities—your distractions. As you watch life fall into place, don't feel bad simply because you've stepped out of the way or given up on the whirlwind of busyness; absenting yourself from certain situations is sometimes the biggest contribution of all.

Sort into three. Divide your distractions into three categories: have to, should, and whatever else can wait. Focus first on what absolutely, positively needs to happen and watch your other tasks practically take care of themselves.

Reconsider the virtues of multitasking. Sometimes doing three things at once actually works. For example, I can help my son with his homework, fix dinner, and turn down a long line of telemarketers all at the same time. On the other hand, I'm an abysmal failure when I try simultaneously to work, do laundry, and return phone calls. Sometimes we absolutely must refrain from doing too many things at once. If you multitask too often, you will miss key points in a conversation, hidden opportunities that require your undivided attention, and the smaller moments that will help you turn what you want into what is yours.

Imagine life without them. Sometimes real living begins when we think of the alternative. It's the same with many parts of our lives; once you imagine life without something, everything seems a little more precious, a bit more illusive. Every so often I wonder how life would be if there weren't so many things vying for my attention. I envision a clear horizon without carpools, dishes, and doctors' appointments. Soon, though, the vision doesn't seem so appealing. The richness of life seems precarious and I slowly realize what a gift some distractions really are.

practice

Sometimes I'm distracted because I don't want to:

1. _____

_____

2. _____

_____

3. _____

_____

If I could, I would eliminate the following distractions:

1. _____

_____

2. _____

_____

3. _____

_____

In some ways I am grateful for my distractions, because:

1. _____

_____

2. _____

_____

3. _____

_____

affirm

Instead of fighting with my busyness and pulling away from all that I do, I celebrate these full days and work at remaining whole.

When I live with my distractions, I

_____

_____

~ week 52 ~

Turn the Life You're Living into the Life You Want

The journey is my home.
—Muriel Rukeyser, "Journey," *One Life* (1957)

ask

1. What is the single most dramatic change I've made over the last year?
2. Where do I want to go now?
3. Will I remain on the same path or select one that's new and uncharted?
4. In what areas have I grown?
5. Do I have any regrets?
6. Am I more confident in my abilities to wish, dream, and do?
7. Have I begun to turn the life I'm living into the life I want?

Over the course of a year you've taken an unusual journey. You've probably asked yourself more questions than you ever thought possible. I hope you've discovered some answers along the way. At the very least, you've learned that growth and change are closely related to your willingness to keep asking. Questions test our beliefs, stretch our intellects, and help us understand where we fit in the world.

Asking questions also leads to movement. One answer carries you to another and another and so on. Before you know it, you've grown and moved closer to your dreams. Integrating the life you're living into the life you want is about asking questions to propel your growth. I like the word *integrate* because it implies a certain unification of all the pieces of your life so that what's important to you is never left out. When you integrate the life you're living into the life you want, you step into that boundless territory where you can always ignite a possibility. As one flame goes out another is illuminated, so that your wishes and dreams are always surrounded by light.

Please don't regard the end of this book as the end of your journey. In many ways, your journey has just begun. The questions, experiments, practice exercises, and affirmations are intended to help you navigate the next part of your journey. But before you move on, contemplate and celebrate all you've learned over the last fifty-one weeks. Think back to a particular circumstance to which you responded with new courage. Pat yourself on the back for all your jobs well done and those that received your best shot. Reexamine old behaviors that were preventing you from taking risks and meeting challenges head-on. Reflect on your spiritual development and gauge your sense of faith in the unknown. Collect your year's worth of miracles and draw on their divine power over the next several months (or longer if you can).

I believe that if we can do the work of our dreams against the backdrop of self-confidence, we are more likely to savor our journeys. We must also have faith in something bigger, a higher being that believes in us even when we don't believe in ourselves. As you wish, dream, and do, you will inevitably face a wide range of hurdles. Amid smooth success, your efforts could be derailed by a host of personal and professional dilemmas. A sick child or parent, an unexpected move, even an old friend who drops by out of the blue can influence the direction, or at the very least the pace, of your journey. If you're in a hurry, these circumstances will slow you down. If you embrace them, however, and give them a place on your path, you will maintain your momentum.

experiment

Celebrate your failures. It's natural to celebrate our successes, but it's just as important to recognize our failures. Remember that a failure is simply a lesson waiting to be learned.

Let your soul breathe. Wishing, dreaming, and doing involve practical matters, but you must let your soul breathe, too. If your spirit doesn't get the oxygen it needs, your efforts to turn what you want into what is yours will fall flat.

Embrace gratitude in the best and worst of times. It's easy to thank your lucky stars when all good things abound. But it's especially rewarding to express your gratitude when the horizon looks bleak. Counting your blessings amid moments of despair can actually enhance your outlook. "Nothing's right" is slowly but steadily replaced with phrases like "Well, I have my health," or, "I'm surrounded by supportive friends," or this old favorite, "Tomorrow is another day." We can be thankful for our tomorrows or the bread on our tables. We can also be grateful for the unexpected opportunities that, at first, appear as disappointments but later turn into blessings.

Choose your authentic self over all others. Other selves will always vie for your attention. The self that doesn't get hurt. The self that has a grip almost all the time. The self that never raises her voice or becomes really angry. But you have many sides—good and bad—that, together, form your authentic self, the one that will accompany you on all your journeys. Choose that self over all others and you will never be alone.

practice

I've begin to inch closer to my dreams by:

1. _____

_____

2. _____

_____

3. _____

_____

My biggest challenges have included:

1. _____

_____

2. _____

_____

3. _____

_____

I am proud to have accomplished:

1. _____

   _____

2. _____

   _____

3. _____

   _____

affirm

I am open to miracles whether they occur with no warning or arrive after a period of hard work.

When I turn the life I'm living into the life I want, I

_____

_____

Start a Wish It Group

As you wish, dream, and do, consider pulling together a group of like-minded people willing to offer support and share ideas. The group could be loosely assembled and remain somewhat fluid, with periodic meetings and even interim e-mails for quick check-ins. You could create a group comprised of people focusing on similar goals; i.e., artists, musicians, bankers, etc. Or you might gather together individuals from different fields to create a cross-pollination of ideas. Just remember to nourish and keep your own wishes and dreams front and center. If you hit a snag, enlist the support of the group. Just make sure that you maintain accountability to your goals. The group dynamic is intended to provide support, but you need to do the work. For more information about Wish It Groups, please visit my web site at www.leslielevine.com

Here's how:

* Invite some friends (friends of friends are okay, too) to form a circle of support using this book as a guide. Enlist people who are good listeners, open-minded, and committed to pursuing their dreams.

* Keep the number to five or six people. That will ensure that everyone gets the support she needs and has adequate floor time during the meetings.

* Meet on a regular basis. Weekly is good, though biweekly or monthly is probably more realistic given people's busy schedules.

* Set firm ground rules covering topics such as confidentiality and meeting format.
* Don't offer unsolicited advice, and use caution and compassion.
* Be honest and forthcoming if someone is not following the guidelines.
* Focus on everyone's strengths.
* Acknowledge everyone's contributions.
* Take turns facilitating.
* Celebrate failures as well as successes.

Suggested Reading

Here are some of books that have inspired and propelled me to wish, dream, and do:

The Artist's Way, by Julia Cameron (Tarcher/Putnam, 1992)

The Carrot Seed, by Ruth Krauss (Harper & Row Publishers, Inc., 1945)

The Comfort Queen's Guide to Life, by Jennifer Louden (Harmony Books, 2000)

Creating a Charmed Life, by Victoria Moran (HarperSanFrancisco, 1999)

Escaping into the Open, by Elizabeth Berg (HarperCollins, 1999)

Everyday Sacred, by Sue Bender (HarperCollins, 1995)

Life Makeovers, by Cheryl Richardson (Broadway Books, 2000)

Living Big, by Pam Grout (Conari Press, 2001)

Making Your Dreams Come True, by Marcia Wieder (Harmony Books, 1999)

Mediations for Women Who Do Too Much, by Anne Wilson Schaef (HarperCollins, 1990)

One Day My Soul Just Opened Up, by Iyanla Vanzant (Fireside, 1998)

Simplify Your Life, by Elaine St. James (Hyperion, 1994)

What the Dormouse Said, collected by Amy Gash (Algonquin Books of Chapel Hill, 1999)

A Woman's Spirit, by the Hazeldén Foundation (HarperCollins, 1994)

Write It Down, Make It Happen, by Henriette Anne Klauser (Scribner, 2000)

Author Contact Information

For more information about Leslie Levine's workshops and appearances, please visit her web site at www.leslielevine.com